Napa Valley Wine History 101

From Wilderness

to

Wine Country

Tim Gaughan Ph.D

ISBN: 978-0-578-05207-6

Press

www.napavalleywinehistory101.com

napavalleywinehistory101@gmail.com

To Debbie and the memory of wine journalist and friend
Jack Heeger.

Acknowledgements

Many people contributed to the development and evolution of this book and helped in various ways. Liz Smith and George Lundberg read very early versions that surely were difficult and even painful to navigate. Lin Weber also read early versions and made excellent suggestions, but in no way is responsible for the historical accuracy of the final product. Jill Decker edited early drafts with great skill.

I am particularly grateful to Sasha Paulsen, editor of the "On Wine" section of the *Napa Valley Register*, for accepting the idea of a six-article series on the history of wine in the Napa Valley which eventually shaped the final form of this book. Rebecca Yerger read early drafts of those articles, and again is not responsible for their historical accuracy. Jack Heeger, *Napa Valley Register* wine columnist and fellow wine tasting enthusiast, also read article drafts and gave me on-the-fly tutoring in journalistic writing techniques. Doug Hattala, a fellow Napa Valley history enthusiast from the Napa Valley Historical Society did a tremendous job on the final edit of the manuscript. Finally, Deborah Dean contributed the illustrations that grace the cover and pages of this book, and has graced my life as my wife and fellow traveler through history for 20 years.

Contents

Chapter I

Overview of Napa Valley Wine History....................................... 7

Chapter II

The Spanish Period... 14

Chapter III

The Mexican Period.. 29

Chapter IV

Wine in the Napa Valley Early in the American Era............... 55

Chapter V

The Establishment of the Wine Industry and Wine Culture of the Napa Valley in the American Era....................................... 85

Chapter VI

Struggles and Triumphs in the Later Period of the American Era.. 108

Chapter I

Overview of Napa Valley Wine History

On a day in 1838, a solitary, grizzled man dressed in buckskin planted a cutting from a grapevine from the Sonoma Valley in the soil of the Napa Valley, and a long journey spanning centuries and thousands of miles was over. A wine grapevine had finally reached the Napa Valley. The vine had been taken from the vineyard of a Mexican government official in Sonoma. It was a "mission" varietal and an ancestor of the *Vitis vinifera* grapevines first planted in California 70 or so years earlier by the Spanish missionary priest Junipero Serra and his followers. *Vitis vinifera*, the wine grape species which was first domesticated in South Caucasus (today Armenia and Georgia) spread gradually throughout Europe and eventually made its way to the New World via the Spanish *conquistadors*. It finally arrived in the Napa Valley and, as we now know, the world of wine would never be the same.

The man doing the planting was George C. Yount, recipient from the Mexican government of the first land grant in the Napa Valley, and the first non-native American resident of the valley. He came to California from across the Sierra Nevada with a party of "mountain men" in 1830. These mountain men were amazingly tough, self-reliant, and independent hunters, trappers, and explorers who not only helped settle the Napa Valley and other parts of California and the West, but also started a chain of events that would change American history dramatically.

The mountain men carved the trails over the Sierra Nevada Mountains to California and guided and aided would-be American settlers in establishing a finger hold in a foreign land that stretched from the Sierras to the shores of the Pacific Ocean. Their incredible adventures soon led to the fulfillment of the idea held at the time by many Americans of "manifest destiny," which ultimately resulted in the United States becoming a world power with land stretching from the Atlantic to the Pacific Ocean. Without the exploits of these extraordinary mountain men, the United States would not have been able to develop into a world power and exert its influence globally, as it has done now for over a century.

George Yount and most of the other mountain men pioneers and the first wave of settlers who crossed the Sierra in wagon trains didn't focus their attention on grape growing and winemaking (while George Yount was the first to plant *vinifera* vines in the Napa Valley, there is no record of him making wine until the Gold Rush brought thousands of thirsty miners—potential consumers of wine—to Northern California in the 1850s). But a small group of men who began to come to the Napa Valley in the 1860s did focus their attention on wine, and they would eventually begin to develop a wine country and wine culture in the valley that is unique and would eventually come to hold an important place in the world of wine.

In the beginning though, the Napa Valley was more about *hats* than grapes and wine. George Yount, and other mountain men who eventually settled in or explored the Napa Valley, were originally attracted to California because of the prospect of hunting for beaver. Julian Pope (for whom Pope Valley is named) and James Clyman (famous for having warned the Donner Party to abandon its planned trip over the Sierras) came to California as mountain men/trappers.

Even the legendary historical western icon Kit Carson briefly passed through some of the valley in search of beaver all the way back in 1829. Beaver felt, the fine, soft, insulating fur found under the outer "guard fur" of the busy little dam-building rodents, produced the material used to make most of the hats in vogue among the upper classes in Europe and the Eastern U.S. at the time.

Beaver felt was the material used to make the hats worn by the 19th century aristocracy, from top hats and derbies to the military and clerical hats worn by the most prominent members of 19th-century society. Because it was in such demand, and beavers were so plentiful in the American West, the daring mountain men risked all in the pursuit of beaver pelts, and they created an industry that was so profitable it yielded America's first tycoon, John Jacob Astor, founder of the American Fur Company for which many a mountain man worked. Unfortunately for the mountain men of Yount, Pope, and Clyman's time, they were so successful at trapping that the beavers almost disappeared from the Western landscape, and these adventurous, independent men had to "retrain" for other occupations like farming, ranching, or tending to orchards or vineyards, often in California.

The mountain men changed the course of American and California history, and one of those men, George Yount, changed the history of the Napa Valley. But he is not really where the story begins. The story goes all the way back to the journey of the *Vitis vinifera* grapevine from the Old World to the New World, which began only a few years after the arrival of Columbus at the close of the 15th century. During the almost two and a half centuries since the coming of Europeans to California, changes in society and government policy during the Spanish, Mexican, and American regimes affected the spread and cultivation of *Vitis vinifera* grapes in California, and eventually in the Napa Valley. There are four areas of California social structure and government policy that most influenced the evolution of viticulture in California, and eventually the Napa Valley: land, trade, immigration, and people.

Land: Land was distributed in different ways by the three countries that had sovereignty over California. During the Spanish period, the Catholic Church owned virtually all of the land in the form of the California missions founded by Father Serra and his followers. Although wine grapes were cultivated virtually from the beginning of the Spanish period, it was only for use in sacramental wine.

While the Spanish failed to establish any missions north of San Francisco (except a small outpost chapel at present-day San Rafael), they planted mission varietal grapevines wherever they would propagate, as the priests came up the coast founding their missions. Thus, modern-day appellations and wine-growing areas such as Santa Barbara, San Luis Obispo/Paso Robles, Monterey, and Santa Cruz owe their beginnings to the Spanish padres of the 18th century.

In the Mexican period, Church land was expropriated by the government, and all of the land not owned by the government was divided into very large *ranchos* that were owned by a small, elite group. Wine grapes were grown outside of the religious community in the Mexican era, but large *rancho* owners did not focus on viticulture or winemaking. Mariano Vallejo, who played a large role in the history of the Napa Valley as the Mexican governor of the territories north of San Francisco, was one of the few Mexicans in California to cultivate wine grapes, and his land in the Sonoma Valley was the source of the vines first planted in the Napa Valley by George Yount.

Finally, during the early American period, these large *ranchos* were broken into smaller parcels which tended to foster agricultural pursuits such as viticulture in places like the Napa Valley. Almost from the beginning of the American period, owing in part to the demand created by the swelling population in the nearby gold fields, vineyards dotted the valley floor.

Trade: Small commercial wine industries emerged in Argentina, Chile, Peru, and New Spain (Mexico) itself relatively soon after Spanish colonization in the 16th century. In California, a remote province of Mexico, however, serious exploration of the land by the Spaniards did not even begin until the 18th century, and during the entire Spanish period, California was extremely isolated. Also, during the Spanish era, no trade with the outside world was allowed by the government. Only a very modest amount of trade between California and Mexico took place, and so there was no large market for wine or any other agricultural products.

The Mexican era saw the introduction of trade in California, although it was quite limited on the Mexican side to products related to livestock, especially cattle. But the very first example of commerce in wine in California occurred during the 27-year reign of the Mexicans in California. A Frenchman from Bordeaux named Jean-Louis Vignes arrived in California in 1831, purchased land on the Los Angeles River, and, in 1840, made the first recorded shipment of California wine. (As galling as it may be to Northern Californians that the first commercial wine shipment in California originated in the southland, it is even more difficult to accept that its destination was the much more populous north, and that Vignes soon made regular shipments to Monterey and the settlement that eventually came to be named San Francisco.)

The Americans opened all avenues of trade to California—trade within California—with the rest of the United States, and trade with the other countries of the world. But a local "instant market" for Napa Valley wine miraculously presented itself with the Gold Rush, and the eventual creation of nearby San Francisco, the first major population center on the west coast of North America (which had a substantial component of immigrants from wine-loving European countries to boot!).

George Yount began making wine for the 49ers from his vineyard of mission grapes, and was joined during the early years of the American era in California by men with names like Patchett, Osborn, Thompson, Pellet, and Crane. These were people whose names are now mostly relegated to the history books, but they struggled mightily to establish the Napa Valley as a source of quality wine for local and national markets. Eventually in the American era, a wine industry emerged, and a healthy wine trade developed.

Immigration: No immigration to California was allowed during the Spanish era other than from Spain or Mexico, and migration from Mexico was limited to the clergy that founded and controlled the missions, a small number of soldiers, and an even smaller number of civilian settlers. During the Mexican era, immigration laws were liberalized, and some foreign immigrants coming by land and sea were allowed to become Mexican citizens and own land. George Yount in the Napa Valley and Jean-Louis Vignes and a group of 20 or so French immigrants who followed him to Southern California are examples of what a more liberal immigration policy did to advance the slow evolution of the cultivation of grapes and the making of wine in Mexican California.

During the American era, all immigrants from the United States and many people from foreign countries were welcomed to California. Immigrants to California during the American era became both producers and consumers of wine from the Napa Valley and other parts of the state.

People: Each era of Californian history brought with it a unique society and type of people. The Spanish era featured a small, domineering clergy, the military, and a very small civilian population that was drawn from the lower classes of New Spain. No market for wine was possible in the Spanish era. During the Mexican era, an oligarchy arose among the people who came to be known as *Californios*. The lifestyle of these oligarchs in some ways appeared to be quite idyllic, but it has also been characterized by some historians as an aimless. Also, California society during the Mexican period included small groups of more ambitious and entrepreneurial pioneers and settlers who drifted in primarily from the United States across the Sierra Nevada. Only a very small trade in wine resulted.

The American period, which began right around the time of the

Gold Rush, brought a variety of people from all over the United States and other parts of the world who came seeking their fortune and/or a new life in California. The social forces at play and the kinds of people that were attracted to California (and eventually the Napa Valley) during the Mexican and American periods had their influence on the evolution of viticulture and winemaking.

At the beginning of the American era in Californian history, land distribution practices, trade, immigration policies and an exploding population of Gold Rush immigrants from the U.S. and all over the world finally made conditions right for a burgeoning wine industry to emerge in the Napa Valley. It was at this critical time in the history of the Valley that a Prussian immigrant named Charles Krug arrived on the eastern shores of the U.S.

It took Krug another decade or so to find the Napa Valley. However, when he did, he established a winery and viticultural practices that are to this very day important parts of the Napa Valley wine culture. Krug was followed closely by a German immigrant, Jacob Schram, and then over the next two decades by German immigrants Jacob and Frederick Beringer and Gustave Niebaum of Finland.

Together, these five immigrants from Europe would end up leaving a legacy that would define the wine culture of the Napa Valley all the way up to the present day. The Napa Valley wine experience is unique, different from all of the other wine areas in the world, and the Napa Valley has its own wine culture that has evolved over the nearly 175 years since the first wine grapevines were planted there. In order to enjoy and appreciate the Napa Valley wine experience to the fullest, an understanding of the valley's wine culture and how it evolved over time is essential. In the chapters that follow, you will learn what you need to know to make your trip to the Napa Valley wine country the most rewarding experience possible based on all that the valley has to offer you.

Chapter II

The Spanish Period

The Napa Valley was first discovered and explored by people of European ancestry in 1823, shortly after Spain had surrendered the territory following Mexico's successful revolution in 1821. Technically, Spain had no direct influence on viticulture in the Napa Valley, and, in fact, didn't know of its existence. But it was the Spanish who first cultivated Old World *Vitis vinifera* grapevines and introduced primitive winemaking techniques in California. It was also the colonial policies and the society that developed in California during the Spanish era (up until 17 years before the valley was first occupied and grapevines were introduced) that provide the historical context for the unique story of wine in the Napa Valley.

Mexico and California under Spain: 300 Years and One Grape Varietal?

Christopher Columbus on his voyage to the New World in 1492 carried wine (probably from the Jerez area of Spain) as part of the provisions for the ship's crew. The provisions on Spanish ships of the day consisted of such consumables as olive oil, honey, nuts, and preserved fish and meat. Wine was also an important part of the sailor's diet. It is certain, however, that Columbus did not bring *Vitis vinifera* vines with him on his voyage because he was expecting to establish a trade route to Asia rather than to discover

14

the New World full of souls to convert and the necessity on the part of the Catholic Church for sacramental wine.

Wine grapevines from Europe were introduced to North America just two decades after the voyage of Christopher Columbus in 1492. Spain itself had been involved with cultivating vines and making wine since the Phoenicians occupied it around 1100 BC. In fact, scholars agree that grapes have been cultivated on Spanish soil since between 4000 and 3000 BC. Through the centuries, the Spanish experimented with numerous varietals and styles of wine, but because the climate is generally quite hot in Spain, its wines did not have a reputation of distinction in the European wine trade around the time of Columbus. Exceptions included the sweeter wine from around Jerez called "sack" (which eventually evolved into Sherry), and wines from around the ports of Cadiz and Malaga.

It is also important to remember that at the time of the discovery of the New World, the established church of Spain was the Catholic Church, where wine was an indispensable part of the celebration of the Mass. Consequently, it is no surprise that very shortly after the Spanish conquest of the Aztecs (and the beginning of their attempts at converting indigenous people in a land where native grapevines thrived but made unpalatable wine), the *conquistadors* introduced Old World *vinifera* wine grapes and established policies about cultivating vines.

Native people were the first producers of wine in the Americas. In the pre-Columbian age (before the arrival of the Spanish *conquistadors*) the Indians used a native North American grapevine to produce a drink to which they added other fruits and honey. Nowadays, in some regions of Mexico, the wine, called "acachul," is still produced. Fernando Cortez and his *conquistadors* discovered that grape species other than *Vitis vinifera* were native to Mexico, but they proved to be unsatisfactory for making wine due to their unpleasant taste. In 1522, a scant year after the conquest, the records indicate that Cortez sent to Spain for vine cuttings.

The first vineyards of *vinifera* grapes in the New World were planted by the Spanish for the Catholic missions in Mexico. Winemaking using grapes from *vinifera* vines began in 1524, when Cortez, then governor of New Spain, ordered every Spaniard with a land grant from the crown to plant 1,000 grapevines for every 100 Indians under his control. It is unknown to this day which European varietal of vine was brought from Spain to Mexico. But the early Spanish in Mexico often described the grapes it produced as "common black grapes" lacking in any distinctive flavor, and eventually came to be known in North America as the "mission" varietal. In South America, they became known as the "criolla" varietal. Mission grapes are still grown today in California and elsewhere.

The Spaniards in Mexico were quite successful in their viticulture endeavors—in fact, too successful. After the defeat of the Spanish Armada in 1588, Spain experienced a continuing decline in economic power and looked to its colonies in the New World as a destination for Spanish exports. King Phillip II outlawed new plantings or vineyard replacements in Mexico after 1595 in order to protect the Spanish wine trade. Some wineries did manage to continue, but no wine industry emerged in Mexico.

The ban on commercial vineyards and winemaking was renewed and upheld for 150 years. It prevented any significant commercial wine industry from developing in Mexico. Priests in the missions did continue with vineyards and produced small amounts of sacramental wine and wine for their personal consumption. And missionaries spreading out to more and more remote places like Baja California brought mission vine cuttings with them so they could produce their own sacramental wine. Some of the wineries or missions that managed to cultivate vines and produce wine, despite the prohibition by Spain, must have introduced other varietals during this long period, but they were of no historical consequence. It was left to 20th and 21st-century Mexican vintners in places like the Valle de Guadalupe in Baja California to prove that Mexico is capable of producing a number of excellent wines.

The Spanish in California: Viticulture and Wine but no Wine Commerce

With that historical backdrop, one would not expect that the Spanish era would result in much in the way of development of viticulture in California, and that is true with one very big exception. The Spanish did bring mission grapevines and introduced viticulture and a primitive form of winemaking to California. Incredibly though, this did not happen until over 200 years after Cortez first planted his mission grapes in Mexico. And neither the vines nor the padres ever made it as far as the Napa Valley in the half-century that the Spanish actually occupied California.

Before looking at the history of wine during the Spanish era in California, it is useful to look at an overview of the most important attributes of California society from the time that the Spanish seriously began to occupy the territory in 1769. That is when Junipero Serra and the other missionaries moved into California, and the Spanish remained there until their rule ended with the Mexican War of Independence (1810-1821). These attributes of society in California prevailed throughout the Spanish period of activity and rule in California.

Land: When the Spanish began to seriously colonize California, their motives were to establish a defensive military position against potential encroachment by other countries like Russia and England. But the Spanish also viewed the conversion and "civilizing" of the native peoples of California as perhaps their most important goal. Thus, it was the missionary priests who took the lead in solidifying Spanish sovereignty over California. As a result, the land of California was put exclusively in the hands of the Church. The military created small forts, and there were a few civilian villages set up with a few large landholdings ("ranchos") also coming into existence. Other than that, *all* of the land that was settled by the Spanish was owned by the Catholic Church. Consequently, massive areas of land were used only for the purpose of hosting missions and recruiting local Indians who were to be converted to Catholicism. There was virtually no large-scale agriculture or any other productive land use during the Spanish era. With the Church having a monopoly on the land, there was almost no secular use of the land either. With very few exceptions, the Spanish civilians who came to California did not own land or engage in any significant agriculture or other economic activity.

Trade: The Spanish "pioneers" in California were extremely isolated, and even if there were any outside contact, trade was not allowed by the Spanish government. The missions were completely self-sufficient. The Indians did all the work to provide for the needs of the missions, and no commerce whatsoever evolved during the Spanish era. As a consequence, California was totally insular during the Spanish era, save for some small amount of contact with the Spanish in New Spain.

Immigration: Given the perceived need to defend California from outsiders, the immigration policies in California prohibited anyone other than a small number of Spanish priests, soldiers, and civilians from immigrating into California. Thus, while the American society on the East Coast of the continent benefited from a continuous influx of people from Europe, because of immigration policies and the isolation of the place, California in the Spanish era had a small and rather stagnant population.

People: The civilians who came to California from New Spain tended to be people from the very lowest classes of Mexican society. It was very difficult to reach California from Mexico City, and there were no economic rewards for doing so. Consequently, people from the aristocracy did not come, and the civilians who did were not very enterprising, owing to the fact that the Spanish system in California focused on the missions and provided little incentive for civilians to develop a civil society.

In 1769, Father Junipero Serra, a Franciscan priest working on behalf of the Catholic Church and the Spanish government, established a mission in what is now San Diego. His goal was to Christianize the indigenous people and attempt to counter the threat to California that the Spanish felt from settlements of Russians and English to the north. Serra brought mission grapevines with him to San Diego and planted them there. From then until they founded their final mission in San Rafael in the 1800s, Serra and his followers carried mission vines for the production of sacramental wine and planted them wherever they would propagate and thrive.

Serra founded eight missions himself, each with an adjacent vineyard. By being the first to bring *Vitis vinifera* vines to California, it can be said that Serra had as much to do with the ultimate development of the California wine industry as anyone, and he is commonly called the "Father of the California Wine." But given the Spanish approach to settling California, Father Serra's contribution to wine in California turned out to be less significant than it could have been under different circumstances. The Spanish efforts to colonize California were far from totally successful. Their grand plan was to organize a series of missions to convert, train, and "civilize" the Indians, a small number of forts to accommodate the military, and an even smaller number of villages of immigrant people from Mexico. The final product was not enough to make California a secure territory of the Spanish Empire.

Historian Leon G. Campbell says: "During the entire Spanish era, the settlements in California were among the smallest outposts of Spanish America, populated by poor, unskilled, largely illiterate members of the lowest strata of Mexican society. Some South American cities at the time of Serra's moving to California had populations in excess of 100,000 persons, ... Yet census figures show that as of 1781, the four presidios, two pueblos, and 11 missions of the province of *Alta California* were populated by no more than 600 persons exclusive of the indigenous groups."[1]

In addition to there being so few people in California during the Spanish era, the people who were there were definitely not highbred

Spanish. Campbell notes: "The first *Californios* were largely non-whites, or *mestizos* of mixed Spanish and Indian parentage, drawn from the towns of northern Mexico or forcibly conscripted from the jails of the same regions to relieve overcrowded conditions. Men of wealth could not be expected to make the journey (to California) ...the hardships were many and the chances of material gain small."[2]

This explains why, although the missionaries introduced grapevines and wine to California, nothing even resembling wine commerce for California wine or other products arose in the Spanish era. The Spanish also implemented two policies concerning their California territory that severely restricted the development of any kind of wine market. First, trade with anyone from outside California was forbidden by Mexico City. Smuggling along the coast with ships coming from several countries did occur, and these rules were eventually relaxed, but they meant that no serious import or export wine business could develop in the territory. Second, the Spanish government gave out almost no land grants for either military people or civilians during its rule in California, instead keeping all productive land for the Catholic Church. Obviously, even if there were a market for wine in California, no one would have any land upon which to plant vineyards commercially.

So the Spanish, due to their weak attempt at the settling of California, their restrictive land, trade, and immigration policies, and the kind of population that arrived from New Spain, effectively eliminated wine as a part of the life of Spanish California. Wine only existed for sacramental purposes and the personal consumption of the missionary priests. When the Spanish period in California ended with the conclusion of the Mexican War of Independence in 1821, California had been introduced to viticulture and wine by the missionary priests, the Napa Valley was still waiting to be discovered, and no wine trade or wine industry seemed likely any time soon.

Because of Spain's policies about vineyard development in Mexico, only the mission varietal of grapevine made it to California. The rather undistinguished mission grape would be adopted by future vintners in the Napa Valley and elsewhere in California and would go on to dominate viticulture and the image of Napa Valley and California wines until the 1880s, over a century after the Spanish priests first began to plant them in California. The early, enlightened Napa Valley vintner Charles Krug criticized his contemporaries for continuing to cultivate the mission varietal, saying that the very ordinary and undistinguished wines that it produced tarnished the reputation of the burgeoning Napa Valley wine industry. Thus the mission grape, Father Serra's indirect contribution to the Napa Valley's wine culture, proved to be quite a mixed blessing.

Chapter II Appendix:

People, Places, and Things in the Spanish Period

Although Spain did not begin to occupy Alta California until 1769, it had claimed the territory as part of New Spain (Mexico) for almost 250 years prior to that. The Spanish government was in California for only 51 years when it was displaced by the Mexican government. The experience of the Spanish with wine in Mexico was to have a major impact on the history of wine in California and eventually the Napa Valley.

Pre-Columbian Wine

In the pre-Columbian age, the Indians used native North American grapevines called "cimarrones" to produce a drink to which they

added other fruits and honey. The wild vines produced lots of grapes, but they were considered by the Spanish to be too acidic to make wine. Nowadays, in some regions of Mexico, the wine called "acachul" is still produced and bottled from wild grapes and fruits.

European Vitis Vinifera in Mexico and South America

Christopher Columbus Discovers the New World

- *Vitis vinifera's journey towards a rendezvous with the Napa Valley started when the Spanish conquistadors began exploring and conquering the New World. We know that the three famous ships led by Christopher Columbus on his voyage to the New World in 1492 carried wine but no vines because he was expecting to establish a trade route to Asia rather than to discover the New World.*

- *The first vineyards of European grapes in the New World were planted by the Spanish conquistadors for the Catholic missions in Mexico. Soon after the Europeans arrived in the New World, they discovered that grape species other than Vitis vinifera were native to North America. They were unsatisfactory to the Spanish for making wine due to their unpleasant taste. Hernando Cortez realized immediately that the Spanish would need wine for the*

23

Catholic mass and requested grapevines from Spain in 1522, one year after the conquest. All of the wine made by the Spanish in the New World came from the European Vitis vinifera grape. Some claim that hybridization took place with native, non-vinifera vines along the way. It is unclear to this day what variety of Vitis vinifera vine was brought from Spain to the New World, but the grapes it produced eventually came to be known in North America as the "mission" variety, and as the "criolla" variety in South America after the late 1500s, when Spanish settlers and missionaries took Mexican vines with them to Peru, Chile, and Argentina. Mission grapes are still grown today in California and elsewhere. Although other varietals were eventually introduced in South America, mission grapes prevailed in Mexican, and eventually, California winemaking throughout the Spanish period.

Casa Madero Winery Today

• *The oldest winery in the Americas was founded at Parras, 130 miles west of Monterrey, Mexico, near the Mission Santa Maria. Casa Madero was founded in 1597 as the San Lorenzo hacienda. Some claim that the quality of the wine that was produced in this area was so good it led the King of Spain to ban the production of wine in Mexico, except for sacramental purposes, in order to protect winemakers in Spain. The Jesuit priest Father Juan Ugarte went north from Parras founding other mission and planting grapevines. At the Loreto mission in Baja California in 1701, he planted the first vines on the Baja peninsula. Jesuit priests established the Mission de Santo Tomas in Baja California in 1791, about 90 miles south of present-day San Diego. Most books attribute the establishment of mission grapevines in California with the planting of vines brought from Baja California by Father Serra to the new mission in San Diego around the year of its founding in 1769. Writer Thomas Pinney, in his excellent "History of Wine in America," argues that the priest in the missions of California actually imported wine from Mexico or Spain for at least a decade after their arrival in California. Taking into consideration the time required for vinifera vines to mature and yield grapes, he points to 1782 and the mission at San Juan Capistrano as California's first vintage. Regardless of where or when the first California vintage occurred, viticulture remained exclusively in the hands of the missionary priests throughout the Spanish period.*

Wine in California in the Spanish Era

• *By being the first to bring Vitis vinifera vines to California, it can be said that Junipero Serra had as much to do with the ultimate development of the California wine industry as anyone. But given the Spanish approach to settling California, Father Serra's contribution to wine in California turned out to be less significant than it could have been under other circumstances.*

• *After all of the neglect of California by the Spanish, late in the 18th century they finally devised a strategy for its settlement and development. The strategy involved the creation of a small number of presidios (military forts), pueblos (civilian villages), and most importantly, missions.*

Monument to the Presidio at Santa Barbara

1. __The Military Presidios:__ The Spanish military was to establish a series of forts—significantly fewer in number than the missions—to protect the territory from military threats. These forts were designed to eventually become the backbone of the military defense system of Spain in California. With scarce financial resources in New Spain and with soldiers reluctant to take posts in the frontier area of California, the series of presidios, like the series of missions, did not meet the expectations of the Spaniards.

U.S. Stamp Commemorating the Establishment of the Pueblo at San Jose

2. __The Pueblos:__ The Spanish intended to establish a network of small communities (pueblos) of civilian pioneers from New Spain to settle in California (San Diego, Los Angeles, San Jose, and San Francisco were sites where pueblos were established). But again, like people in the military, settlers were reluctant to leave New Spain to settle in California, and the pueblo system never really took hold during the Spanish era.

From a Historical Photo of the Mission in Santa Clara

3. __The Missions:__ Serra and the Franciscan priests worked to establish a series of religious missions which were about one day's travel apart up the California coast. Serra built nine missions

27

within 15 years and they extended up the California coast from San Diego to San Rafael. (Eventually there were 21 missions extending as far as the mission at Sonoma, which wasn't completed until the mid-1800s after the Spanish had departed California.) While founding their missions, the Franciscans planted mission grapevines wherever they would propagate. By the early 1800s, vines were grown at the Southern California missions and as far north as the mission at Santa Clara. The mission priests vinified using cowhides stitched together to hold the grapes, which were crushed underfoot, usually by the mission Indians. The juice then went into whatever receptacle was available for fermentation.

None of these three approaches by the Spanish resulted in California being either settled or developed in any meaningful sense. But at least their efforts resulted in Vitis vinifera vines making it as far as Northern California. Every new mission established by the Spaniards represented a new frontier for Vitis vinifera. Vineyards that can be traced back to the missions are still to be found in many places in California, and the missionaries planted vines in many of today's grape-growing areas like Santa Barbara and San Luis Obispo which now help to make California a world-famous producer of wine. It wasn't until 1824, when Mexican Padre Jose Altimira planted several thousand grapevines, that vineyards came to the northerly most of the missions, Sonoma.

Chapter III

The Mexican Period

In the beginning of the 19th century, the 300-year Spanish rule in the New World began to crumble. In 1810, Simón Bolívar began a revolt in Venezuela against Spain. He was defeated twice and was forced to flee to the Caribbean, but in 1817, he reentered Venezuela and succeeded in being the first to overthrow the Spanish in the New World. From that point until about 1825, wars of independence continued in Latin America and eventually ended the Spanish Empire there.

In Mexico in 1810, the beginning of the end for the Spanish was the famous call for their overthrow by the Mexican priest Miguel Hidalgo, and Mexican independence came in 1821. As California was so remote from the capital in Mexico City, it took some time for the word to reach there and for the new Mexican authorities to consolidate their power and begin to create a new government. In 1825, after several years of local provisional government, California formally became a territory of Mexico. The Mexicans, like the Spanish, did not do very much to "develop" California during the following 22 years of their rule over the territory. California remained an isolated outpost, with very few Mexicans residing there and few Mexicans coming north from the center of Mexico to increase the population. Also during the Mexican era, the indigenous population continued to decline rapidly due to disease and maltreatment by the

Mexicans. Sadly, some immigrants from America also contributed significantly to the decimation of indigenous groups in California during the Mexican period.

Although the Mexican government had no interest in or knowledge of the developments surrounding wine in California, the new policies they introduced concerning land ownership, trade, and immigration in California and the blend of people that came to live here during this period led to a surprising number of landmark developments in the history of wine in California, especially considering that the Mexicans ruled there for only 27 years.

New Policies and Changes in California Society During the Mexican Period

Land: The lands owned by the missions where virtually all the viticulture had taken place during the Spanish period were expropriated and put in private hands through government land grants. Although poor people from the lower strata of the society of New Spain had come to populate Spanish California, these new land use laws introduced by the Mexicans quickly gave rise to a powerful landed class in California. Government officers, previously wealthy landholders from Mexico, and a fortunate few from California and central Mexico, as well as other countries, quickly filled the void and became landed *Californios* during the Mexican period from 1821 to 1846. As a consequence, the *"Californio Rancheros"* (landowning Mexican citizens of California) lived on huge "ranchos" (very large parcels of land granted by the government). Besides drastically changing landowning patterns in California, this made secular viticulture possible, and some did indeed appear, though mostly thanks to immigrants who came from outside of California. Land grants were given to both the *Californio* residents of Mexico and the immigrants, and in many cases, these two groups behaved quite differently, especially when it came to using the land for wine production.

Trade: *Californios,* along with newly arrived immigrants, were now allowed to trade with the outside world as well as within California, whereas the Spanish before them were prohibited from trading with foreigners and traded among the missions, and almost not at all with central Mexico. Foreign merchants with finished products from the East Coast of America came to California from around Cape Horn in ships to trade for hides and tallow primarily. The finished goods they brought effectively put a stop to any manufacturing in California, thus perpetuating the *Californio* culture. Grapevines and wine were traded around California for the first time. The prospect of trade also brought trappers and traders from the United States and adventurers from other parts of the world to California. Many of them stayed and began to engage in agriculture. A few pursued viticulture and established a burgeoning wine trade.

Immigration: The Mexicans allowed Americans and others to come to California, and in many cases gave them large land grants. On the northern frontier of California, the Mexican government officials often welcomed immigrants because the Mexicans still couldn't induce capable people to come to California from the heart of Mexico. It was thought that foreigners with large landholdings would act as a buffer between the northern provinces of Mexico and the Russians and the British, who had settlements north of California.

People: During the Mexican era, the kind of people to be found in California changed drastically. The missionary priests were expelled and the Church no longer had a significant role to play. Priests were now relatively unimportant in Californian society, compared to what they were during the days of Father Serra. A group of Mexican elite (the *Californios*) took over the land that had belonged to the Church, converted it into vast landholdings called *ranchos* and became the predominant social class. The regional governments and military troops remained fairly small, but many senior government and military officers acquired large *ranchos*, and with them great wealth and influence. The lower classes originally from Mexico and the indigenous Californians worked for the *rancheros* and made no significant contribution that was recorded in the history of California during the Mexican era. No major population centers arose, and Los Angeles, Monterey, San Jose, and the future San Francisco were the only Mexican settlements to speak of. Meanwhile, a group of pioneers and settlers, mostly from American frontier states like Missouri, began to trickle in and make a significant impact on California's society, bringing with them ambition and the entrepreneurial spirit. There was a new dynamism at work in California as a result of three factors: the mix of new Mexican landed elites and immigrants from the U.S. and elsewhere, the abandonment of the missions and the wine they produced, and the abundance of land available for settlement. This situation led to events and trends in the story of wine in California and the Napa Valley that could not have been predicted and that make for fascinating history.

The Rise of the Californio Culture

Secularization of the missions was a result of Mexico's extreme distrust of the Catholic Church. The Church was an institution that the new Mexican government viewed to be so closely aligned to Spain as to threaten Mexico's newly won independence.

During the Spanish missionary period in California, winemaking had gradually increased to the point where the missions were producing thousands of barrels of wine, although virtually all of it was consumed within the mission system. (Quite a lot of wine to be used strictly for communion, but that's what historians tell us!) One of the important changes made by the new Mexican government was to secularize the missions in California. As these were the only sources of wine, mission vineyards gradually secularized, disappeared, or in some cases were even destroyed by the priests themselves in retribution. But even though the wines made at the missions by the Franciscans eventually disappeared with the fall of the Spanish, the Mexican period proved to be at least somewhat beneficial for vineyard planting and winemaking in California.

The Mexican government also drastically changed the land distribution laws of California, and, as a result, a nascent secular viticulture began to emerge. The Spanish policy generally was not to issue land grants to anyone—civilian or military—that came to California during their rule. The new Mexican government not only took the land away from the missions, but it also made that land and other unclaimed land available to individuals. Most of the missions' lands were disposed of in large grants given to *Californios* or selected recently arrived immigrants to California mostly from the U.S. These land grants were typically for very large parcels of land and gave rise to the *rancho* economy and lifestyle enjoyed by large landholders.

In the ten years before the missions were dismantled, the Mexican government issued only 50 grants for large *ranchos*. In the dozen years after the missions were secularized, 600 new grants were made. The new land grant policies that came as a result of the secularization of the missions were to have a dramatic impact on not only the areas formerly controlled by the missions, but also areas of California—like the Napa Valley—that were not previously under the influence of the missions during the Spanish period.

With all of the mission land now liberated by the Mexican government, a new landed class of Mexicans, who came up to California from mainland Mexico, as well as people already living in California who rose through society to acquire land, created a new economy and culture. As one author noted: "A new culture sprang up now in California: the legendary life of the *ranchero* and his family in a society where cattle-raising and the marketing of beef and hides became the central factors of economic life. With the end of the missions, most local attempts at manufacturing stopped. The California ranchers, their lands generally close to the Southern California coast, became more and more dependent on the goods brought by the foreign merchants who came in search of hides."[3]

These *Californios* created a culture that was seemingly more conducive to viticulture than that of the Spanish. However, because the "monopolistic" role of the church had been eliminated and land was secularized, it did not turn out to advance it that much. Some of these landholders did not plant vines to make wine. One of the rare landholders in Northern California who did plant vineyards was Mariano Vallejo, the governor of the Sonoma territory, who plays a huge role in the development of the Napa Valley and in Californian history in general.

But more important than the *Californios* and their *ranchos* to the development of viticulture in California and the Napa Valley were the *foreigners* who also received land grants from the Mexican government. There were few permanent non-Hispanic residents before Mexican independence, but their numbers increased steadily in the Mexican era. By the early 1840s, California had a native population of less than 100,000 with some 14,000 other permanent residents. Of these, perhaps 2,500 were "foreigners," whites of non-Hispanic descent, and of these, probably 2,000 had emigrated from the United States prior to 1840. The new policies implemented by the Mexicans served as a magnet to attract foreigners, primarily from the United States. Some of these foreigners settled in the Napa Valley and became the early pioneers of the wine industry.

The Early Life and Times of George C. Yount

There is no better way to track the history of wine in California during the Mexican era than to tell the story of George Yount, the first person of European descent to settle in the Napa Valley, and the first to plant grapevines of European descent there. While Yount, for whom the town of Yountville is named, is a fairly well-known figure and several books have been written about him, the historical significance of his experience coming to and living in California remains rather unappreciated. As a result of his adventures as mountain man, explorer, and pioneer settler, he had firsthand experience with many of the people who made California wine history during the Mexican period as well as the early American period. And he made a bit of wine history himself, even though wine seemingly was not a matter of any interest to him at all until much later in his life.

Yount was born in North Carolina in 1794, and when he was a young child, his family moved to Missouri. At age 24, he married his wife, Eliza, who was only 15. He developed a case of wanderlust and, after several long trips away from his wife, he sold almost everything that he had, left to travel west, and never saw her again.

Because of Mexico's liberalized policies towards trade and immigration, groups of Americans and others began to travel to Mexican soil, primarily to trade, hunt, and trap beaver. The starting point for most of these expeditions was New Mexico, another desolate outpost of Mexico inherited from the Spanish. After hearing reports about the wonders of California, Yount, who now had several wilderness adventures under his belt, determined to become a mountain man and joined an expedition led by William Wolfskill, a very capable and experienced wilderness explorer, hunter, and trapper.

Wolfskill and his party of approximately 20 trappers left New Mexico in September 1830. Wolfskill's idea was to follow the Old Spanish Trail trapping beaver along the way, and then take the pelts via the Trail to the small *pueblo* of Los Angeles, where they could be sold to one of the merchant ships from the U.S. or other countries that engaged in trade along the California coast during the Mexican era. Simply by arriving in Los Angeles from Santa Fe using the Old Spanish Trail all the way, the Wolfskill party made history. It is credited with opening the Old Spanish Trail for thousands of future immigrants who later migrated to Southern California during the Mexican and early American periods of California. Several mountain men—some who would eventually impact the history of the Napa Valley in one way or another—had used segments of the Old Spanish Trail as routes of transportation for their beaver trapping trips, but the Wolfskill Party was the first to span the entire Trail. Antoine Robidoux, a Frenchman who, after returning from California to Missouri, held many town hall meetings enticing lots of people (like Joseph Chiles, who was the first to settle in Chiles Valley) to come to California, trapped beaver along segments of the Old Spanish Trail. Jedediah Smith, the most famous of all of the mountain men, and the first to cross the Sierra into Northern

California providing a route for future settlers of the Napa Valley, trapped along segments of the Trail, as well, and the legendary Kit Carson, who had actually explored the Napa Valley on a hunting trip the year before the Wolfkill Party, and would go on to serve with many Napa residents under John C. Fremont in the California Brigade during the Mexican War, did so as well. The Wolfskill Party arrived in Southern California in early 1831. Some of the men in the party decided to return to New Mexico, but Wolfskill and Yount decided to go on to the coast. Without having a trade or any idea of where he wanted to live, Yount went with Wolfskill to the coast, where they built a large sloop, believed to be the first boat of its size ever built in California, and hunted otters all the way up to near San Luis Obispo. When Wolfskill said he wanted to return to Southern California, Yount decided to go north instead. The two parted company and never saw each other again.

What importance does George Yount's relationship with William Wolfskill have to the evolution of wine in California and the Napa Valley? As it turns out, Wolfskill was an American who became a mountain man and came to California because the prospect of trade, and when he got there, he took advantage of the new Mexican laws regarding land ownership and became a pioneer of viticulture in Southern California. After acquiring land from the Mexican government, where downtown Los Angeles now stands, Wolfskill began a large agricultural business growing grapevines. He eventually planted 32,000 vines on a 48-acre vineyard, planting mission vines initially and experimenting with other varietals later. Buy the time of his death in 1866, he was producing 50,000 gallons of wine per year. He was by far the greatest producer of table grapes in California during the Mexican era. He was also a pioneer in citrus agriculture, and in 1857, he became the first man to plant and grow oranges commercially in California. He eventually came to own the world's largest orange grove of the day and established Southern California as a citrus capital. He is recognized by many historians as not only a pioneer of California wine, but also of California agriculture in general.

If we go one degree of separation from George Yount via Wolfskill, we encounter his neighbor, friend, and business rival in the tiny pueblo of Los Angeles, the French immigrant Jean-Louis Vignes. Because of Mexico's newly liberalized trade and immigration policies, a group of French settlers came to Southern California and became very important in the early economy of the pueblo of Los Angeles. The best-known viticulturist and winemaker of the group was Vignes. In 1832, he arrived in Los Angeles from Bordeaux and, because of liberalized Mexican land use policies, was able to buy a ranch on the Los Angeles River near Wolfskill's property. In 1833, because of the new trade policies, he was able to get cuttings from a number of varieties of grapevines from Europe, which he grafted onto mission grapevine rootstock. He was the first person to import European vines other than the mission varietal into California. He imported French varietals such as Cabernet Sauvignon, Cabernet Franc and Sauvignon Blanc.

Vignes, a Frenchman with an appreciation of good wine, did this because, although he thought the soil in Southern California was quite good for growing grapes, good wine could not be made from the mission grape. Soon he was making more and better wine than any of the growers in California and is regarded by some as the "father of the wine industry in California." Vignes' El Aliso Winery eventually became one of the largest in the world, producing 150,000 bottles a year, including the first California sparkling wine.

While American mountain men and French immigrants were busy taking advantage of the new Mexican trade, land use, and immigration policies and revolutionizing California grape growing and winemaking in the Los Angeles area, what happened to our hero, George Yount? After leaving Wolfskill, Yount traveled up the coast, meeting at one point with an early California immigrant from the U.S., Thomas Larkin of Monterey. He was acting as U.S. consul to the Mexican province of *Alta California*, and told Yount of the opportunities north of the San Francisco peninsula. Yount continued all the way to the northern frontier beyond the Golden Gate and stopped at the mission at San Rafael, finally going as far as the mission at Sonoma. In Sonoma, he met, befriended, and eventually went to work for Governor Mariano Vallejo, another prominent figure in the history of wine and in the history of Northern California in general during the Mexican period.

Mariano Vallejo was the colorful governor of the Mexican territory that included all land north of today's San Francisco, including Sonoma, the Napa Valley, and the surrounding territory. Vallejo took advantage of the new Mexican land distribution and trade laws and distributed large portions of the former Sonoma Mission to *himself* in the form of a large *rancho*. Eventually, his landholdings totaled 175,000 acres. Like most *Californios* of his stature, Vallejo's huge parcels of land were used primarily for raising cattle—an economically inefficient use of the rich land found in the Sonoma Valley. He also had the lifestyle of the *Californio*, enjoying the bounty of the land under his possession while doing relatively little to develop it. This was very typical of the owners of the huge *Californio ranchos*.

But unlike most other *rancheros* of his time, Vallejo included vineyards in his vast landholdings. He had taken mission grapevines from the San Rafael and Sonoma missions when they were disbanded, and he was one of the few *Californio rancheros* to produce wine. Although it was not the focus of the work on his *rancho*, "(h)e began commercial winemaking in 1839 and his was the first winemaking operation north of San Francisco Bay—and wound up dominating the region's vintners for 25 years."[4]

George Yount endeared himself to Vallejo while in Sonoma, partially by making roof shingles (virtually his only skill outside of hunting and trapping) for Vallejo's home. And in 1836, Mariano Vallejo gave Yount the first land grant in the Napa Valley, a place where Yount had explored previously and told Vallejo he had an interest in. As a part of the new land use policies of the Mexican government and as governor of the northern territory, Vallejo had the permission of the central government to give land grants to people—Americans included— whom he thought would be a benefit to the Mexican government by settling the area north of San Francisco.

Yount named his land grant "Rancho Caymus," and it consisted of 11,814 acres, which today roughly follows Highway 29 and extends from the south slightly above today's Yountville through the Oakville and Rutherford appellations. He did not settle and build on the land until the spring of 1838. Yount brought with him grapevine cuttings most certainly from Mariano Vallejo's vineyard, and soon George Yount found himself right in the middle of wine history again. Napa Valley wine historian Charles Sullivan, who has researched the matter, believes that Yount first planted his vines during the dormant season of 1838-39. The mission grapes he eventually harvested from his small vineyard were the first *Vitis vinifera* grapes ever grown in the Napa Valley.

Partly because his land grant property was so immense, Yount did not engage in any intensive viticulture or any other large-scale agriculture. Instead, like the other *Californios* of his time, he raised some cattle, hunted and fished on his property, and grew a few vegetables (ever the mountain man, Yount always claimed to have a strong dislike for farming). Yount is a perfect example of how the land use, immigration and trade policies of the Mexican period changed the social structure of California and advanced the spread of *Vitis vinifera* grapevine. But at the same time, the size of the typical *rancho* and the lifestyle of the *Californios* in Northern California did not encourage men like George Yount to pursue serious viticulture, at least not in the Mexican period.

While mission grapevines were eventually planted in several places in the Napa Valley during the Mexican period, very few records exist of actual winemaking. Many early pioneers from the U.S. visited Yount at Rancho Caymus during the Mexican period, as he was famously a very welcoming host. None of these people, however, reported drinking wine at a meal with Yount, and there is no record of him ever making wine until the Gold Rush, when everyone in the Napa Valley either dropped everything and headed for the gold fields or began providing products for the throngs of miners, and wine and brandy were certainly popular with them.

George Yount remained on Rancho Caymus and lived until 1865, well into the American period of the history of wine in the Napa Valley, and he continued to be a part of or a witness to wine history. In 1842, he was surprised to find that the brother of an old friend had become a distant neighbor in Solano. Sometime shortly after he arrived and became the first settler in the Solano Valley, John Wolfskill, younger brother of William, became the second American after Yount himself to plant *vinifera* grapes in Northern California. Today John Wolfskill is considered by historians to be the first commercial farmer in Northern California.

Yount's first neighbor in the Napa Valley was Edward Bale, an Englishman who had married Mariano Vallejo's niece and settled on an enormous land grant property that extended north of Rancho Caymus up to today's Calistoga. Although he is on record as having planted some mission vines on his property, he also made little effort developing vineyards. He did sell off portions of his *rancho* to some of the settlers who started to arrive in the Napa Valley by wagon train in the early 1840s. Some of them, such as David Hudson, John York, and Wells Kilburn, have been credited with planting mission grapes and making small amounts of wine on their properties, probably using the primitive techniques of the Spanish missionaries.

Bale did, however, become a part of Napa Valley wine history when his daughter married Charles Krug, the "father of the Napa Valley wine industry." Krug converted the 500 acres of Bale's land that was part of Caroline Bale's dowry into vineyards that are famous to this day. But before that, he is credited with being the Napa Valley's first "wine consultant," making wine for many Napa Valley residents during the early American era. Eventually, one of his clients turned out to be the former mountain man George Yount. As a result of Krug's winemaking prowess, George Yount, the man who would rather hunt or fish than farm on his historical Napa Valley property, became a respected vintner in his later years.

Chapter III Appendix:

People, Places, and Things in the Mexican Period

Like the Spanish, the Mexicans did not do very much to "develop" California during the 22 years of their rule over the territory. California remained an isolated outpost. The Mexicans who were residing there (literally numbering in the hundreds in the whole of California) did little to attract other Mexicans to come north to the territory. However, immigrants from America and elsewhere did arrive and thrive. Also during the Mexican era, the indigenous population continued to decline rapidly due to disease and maltreatment by the Mexicans. Sadly, some immigrants from America also contributed significantly to the decimation of indigenous groups in California during the Mexican period.

Wine and Society in the Mexican Period

Spanish Missions in the Mexican Era

• *The most important change in the development of wine production in California resulting from the change from the Spanish to Mexican periods was the secularization of the missions. The secularization of the missions was a result of Mexico's extreme distrust of the Catholic Church. The Church was an institution that the new Mexican government viewed to be so closely aligned to Spain as to threaten Mexico's newly won independence. In 1827, the Mexican Congress passed the General Law of Expulsion, which resulted in the expulsion of all Spaniards, including priests. In 1833, the Act for the Secularization of the Missions of California officially secularized all the mission property in Mexico.*

- *During the Spanish missionary period in California, winemaking had gradually increased to the point where the missions were producing thousands of barrels of wine, although virtually all of it was consumed within the mission system. The only sources of wine in California, mission vineyards were gradually secularized, disappeared, or in some cases were even destroyed by the missionaries themselves in retribution. While the wines made at the missions by the Franciscans eventually virtually disappeared with the fall of the Spanish, the Mexican period proved to be at least somewhat beneficial for vineyard planting and winemaking in California, thanks in great part to immigrants in Southern California.*

- *The Mexican government also drastically changed the land distribution laws of California, and, as a result, a nascent secular viticulture began to emerge. The Spanish policy was not to issue land grants. The new Mexican government not only took the land away from the missions, but it also made that land and other unclaimed land available to individuals. Most of the missions' lands were disposed of in large grants given to Californios, or selected recently arrived immigrants to California, mostly from the U.S. These land grants were typically for very, very large parcels of land, and gave rise to the rancho economy and lifestyle enjoyed by large landholders.*

- *In the ten years before the missions were dismantled, the Mexican government issued only 50 grants for large ranchos. In the dozen years after the missions were secularized, 600 new grants were made. The new land grant policies that came as a result of the secularization of the missions were to have a dramatic impact on the areas formerly controlled by the missions, but also areas of California—like the Napa Valley—that were not previously under the influence of the missions during the Spanish period. They gave rise to the era of the California Ranchero.*

• *There are some examples of secular wine production in the Mexican period beginning as far back as the 1820s by Californios and foreigners (usually sailors from ships from America and elsewhere). It occurred almost exclusively in the area of the pueblo of Los Angeles, but it was most certainly for local consumption and was such a small volume that it could not be considered to have been wine commerce.*

Mariano Vallejo

• *Mariano Vallejo was a true native Californio, having been born in Monterey in 1808. Later, Vallejo became Military Commander while at the San Francisco Presidio.*

• *Vallejo became the Commandant of Alta California's northern frontier (all of the Mexican land north of San Francisco). After the missions were secularized by the Mexican government, he*

43

established a fort in Sonoma where the last of the California missions called San Francisco de Solano had been.

• *Vallejo became the only person empowered to grant land in the territory north of San Francisco, and was authorized to issue some grants of land to settlers from America and elsewhere, in order to provide a buffer against the Russians at Fort Ross and the British in Oregon.*

• *When it came to land grants, Vallejo issued all of the 14 land grants awarded in the Napa Valley to native Californios and immigrants like George Yount, Edward Bale, and Joseph Chiles. He also took very good care of himself and eventually his landholdings totaled 175,000 acres, used primarily for raising cattle.*

• *Unlike other Californio rancheros, Vallejo did have vineyards (derived from mission varietal vines he took from the missions San Francisco de Solano and San Rafael). He made wine and eventually became one of the most prominent vintners in Northern California in the early American period.*

The Mountain Men Pioneers: Overland from the United States

• *When the Mexicans opened trade in California, the mountain men came to trade, trap, and in some cases, settle. The members of the Wolfskill Party were mountain men, destined to make history by*

opening up an important trade and immigration route to Southern California.. Two of them, William Wolfskill and George Yount would also make history in the development of the California wine industry without any intention of doing so when they left for California. They departed in 1830from New Mexico, (another Mexican territory opened to trade when the Spanish departed) using the Old Spanish Trail which, as its name implies had been used as a trade route from New Mexico to California by the Spanish. Segments of the Old Spanish Trail had been used as routes for beaver trapping sojourns by famous mountain men such as Jedediah Smith, Kit Carson, , and Antoine Robidoux, each of whom in his own way would have an impact on the history of the Napa Valley.

Jedediah Strong Smith

• *The most well known of the mountain men, **Jedediah Strong Smith,** was born January 6, 1799, and his family moved several times in an effort to stay on the edge of the ever-moving frontier. He led the first group of United States citizens to come overland to California in 1826. At the age of 22, he began to travel to the Upper Missouri and trap beaver.*

- *He led a group into the central Rockies through the South Pass: the key to the settlement of Oregon and California, and eventually the Napa Valley. In his lifetime, Smith would travel more extensively in unknown territory than any other single mountain man.*

- *He was the first American to travel overland through the central Rockies, then down to Arizona, across the Mojave Desert and into California, using segments of the Old Spanish Trail.*

- *James Clyman, who later settled in the Napa Valley after a long "career" as a mountain man, not only saved Smith's life but also his scalp on one of their trapping adventures! Smith was attacked by a grizzly bear that broke his ribs, and Smith literally had his scalp ripped off by the bear. When the attack was over, his scalp was hanging onto his head by an ear. Smith told Clyman to find some thread and a needle and sew it back on, which he did.*

Kit Carson

Kit Carson was one of the earliest visitors to the California territory. In 1829, he left on a trapping expedition and during that trip he became the second American to lay eyes on the Napa Valley. In the spring of 1829, Carson signed on with a trapping party of forty men, led by Ewing Young, the business partner of William Wolfskill. After following the Old Spanish Trail, the group headed south into unexplored Apache country along the Gila River. In 1842, Kit Carson joined John Fremont of the United States Army, who was leading a government-sponsored expedition whose goal was to explore the far West—California and Oregon—with the purpose of collecting scientific, geological, and mapping information. It was the first of three such expeditions led by Fremont that Carson participated in. The last of them resulted in Fremont going to Sonoma weeks after the Bear Flag Revolt had taken place, where he replaced the Bear Flag with the Stars and Stripes. He then formed the California Brigade, which was composed mostly of residents of Napa who had participated in the revolt, led them out of Sonoma and into the Napa Valley. There they crossed the Napa River (a plaque commemorating this crossing can be seen in Veteran's Park in downtown Napa) on their way to begin military engagement in the Mexican War, which resulted in California becoming a U.S. possession.

• *Carson's knowledge of the mountains and the terrain of California was essential to the success of Fremont's expeditions. When Fremont published his reports, Kit Carson was heralded as one of the most trusted and respected men in the West, and he became a genuine legend, with stories about his exploits still being told today.*

• *In 1853, after his days as a mountain man and guide, he was appointed as an Indian agent for Taos, New Mexico, and spent the rest of his days there. While several men like Fremont have attested to the frontiersman skills of Carson, there is also a substantial body of evidence of his cruelty to, and even murder of, Native Americans. But he is not at all alone in this. It is well documented that the California Indians were severely brutalized from the time of the arrival of people of European descent beginning with the Spanish priests, soldiers, and civilians in the 18th century on down to early pioneers like Carson and through to the Gold Rush and beyond.*

William Wolfskill

• *William Wolfskill (1798-1866) was born in Kentucky and followed his adventurous heart to the western frontier, where he became a frontiersman and trapper. He came to Taos in what is now New Mexico, where he encountered a number of likeminded men who wanted to go to California. A Mexican trader had made the first commercial roundtrip journey in 1829-1830 along the southern route of what was to be called the Spanish Trail. But it was William Wolfskill "who organized the first commercial pack train of 1830-1831 and inaugurated consistent use of the entire route (Spanish Trail) from 1830-1848," according to the San Luis Valley Museum Association. The Spanish Trail became the main route from the east to Southern California in the Mexican era.*

• *When they had crossed the mountains into California with the other mountain men, William Wolfskill and George Yount together headed for the Southern California coast, where they built a large schooner (said to be the first large vessel built in California) and began hunting otter. They traveled the coast going as far north as San Luis Obispo, but were not very successful with their hunting. It was at this point that Wolfskill decided that he would find some land in Southern California, and Yount decided to go north on a trip that* would eventually find him in the Napa Valley as its first settler.

• *After acquiring land in Southern California from the Mexican government, Wolfskill began a large agricultural business growing grapevines. He eventually planted 32,000 vines on a 48-acre vineyard where he planted mission varietal vines initially and experimented with other varietals later. He was by far the greatest producer of table grapes in California during the Mexican era.*

• *From 1838 on, Wolfskill devoted himself to his vineyards and orchards. He was also a pioneer in citrus agriculture, and in 1857, he became the first man to plant and grow oranges commercially in California. He eventually came to own the world's largest orange grove of the day and established Southern California as a citrus capital, which it remained until the 1950s, when the opening of Disneyland and the spread of the suburbs gradually overran the huge orchards of Orange County.*

John Wolfskill

• *The success of immigrant pioneers in agricultural commerce often attracted others from United States to come to California. This was true of William Wolfskill, for three of his brothers joined him* *and became prominent in early California agriculture themselves. The first brother to join William was **John Wolfskill**. He arrived in Los Angeles in February of 1838, worked for his brother for two years, and finally headed to Northern California to find some property for himself. He found an area that he fell in love with in what is now Solano County, to the east of the Napa Valley near what is now Winters. Wolfskill petitioned Governor Vallejo for a land grant, but at first he was refused. Finally, after a lot of pleading with the governor, a land grant was provided, but in the name of his brother, William. Eventually, the property was deeded over to John after he had worked it for a number of years.*

• *John Wolfskill almost immediately began commercial farming on his land and was the second American after George Yount to plant grapevines in Northern California. He is said to have visited Yount on several occasions, probably out of the need for the company of a fellow American immigrant. Throughout his long lifetime, John engaged in commercial farming that included a wide variety of produce, including orange and apricot fruit trees and assorted vegetables. He also kept a vineyard on his property. Having arrived in Northern California only shortly after George Yount (who was the first American to settle between what is now San Francisco and the Sierras), John Wolfskill is credited with being the first commercial farmer in Northern California. His success inspired his brother Malthus to join him a few years later. In 1852, another brother, Sachel, arrived. He and Malthus eventually established farms of their own near John's. In 1858, another brother, Milton, came to California.*

• *In the Spanish era, no one but the government and Church was allowed to own land. In the Mexican period, land was put in private hands. But the Californios with their large and self-sustaining ranchos had little motivation to promote commercial activities. However, enterprising Americans and immigrants from other countries were attracted to California by the opportunity to acquire land and eventually engage in trade. Thus was established the early environment where viticulture in California, and eventually the Napa Valley, would flourish. William Wolfskill was the early pioneer in Southern California who took advantage of that environment during the Mexican era, and his brother John did the same in Northern California.*

George Yount

- *The story of how Vitis vinifera finally arrived in the Napa Valley and how the Valley was settled and began to grow into a wine region begins with the Napa Valley's first mountain man pioneer, **George Yount**. The first Americans who came to California were the pioneers coming by land or sea, and they were followed by the settlers. Yount was a true mountain man and pioneer who came across the Sierra, explored California extensively from south to north, and then subsequently came to find his way to the Napa Valley.*

- *Yount decided he wanted to live out his life in the Napa Valley, and eventually was given a land grant by Mariano Vallejo, the governor of the northern provinces of Mexican California. Yount built a home for himself and became the first settler of the Napa Valley, as well as the first person to plant Vitis vinifera vines there, vines most certainly given to him by Mariano Vallejo.*

• *Yount was born in North Carolina in 1794, and when he was a young child, his family moved to Missouri. He joined the military during the War of 1812 when he was 18 years old, and he married his wife, Eliza, when she was 15. He left to travel west telling his wife that he would return. After she waited for him for several years, Eliza finally divorced Yount and married another man.*

• *Yount enjoyed not only the land but also the culture of the Californios, and he fit in from the very beginning. When William Wolfskill decided that he would return to Southern California, Yount went to Sonoma and endeared himself to Vallejo by making shingles for Vallejo's home. After being baptized in the Catholic Church, which was a requirement for becoming a Californio and a property holder in Mexican California, Yount was given a land grant by Mariano Vallejo in the Napa Valley in 1836, which he named "Rancho Caymus."*

• *As was the policy of the Mexican government in issuing land grants, the size of Yount's plot of land was immense, and the grants in the Napa Valley that were to follow Yount's were quite large as well. The average size of the 14 Napa Valley land grants from Yount's original grant until that of Joseph Chiles (which was issued in 1844, shortly before the end of the Mexican rule) was 11,250 acres.*

• *Probably in the dormant season of 1838-39, Yount propagated the first Vitis vinifera grapevine in the Napa Valley, ending a more than 300-year journey for Vitis vinifera from the vineyards of Spain to the Napa Valley!*

• ***Antoine Robidoux*** *(not pictured) became one of the primary sources of information about California for people on the western frontier of America in the middle of the 19th century. He returned to Missouri from his trip to California with the Wolfskill Party and spoke to large groups of people at "town hall meetings" about the wonders of California. In 1841, he delivered a speech praising California in the town of Weston, Missouri, which inspired John Bidwell to mount the first covered wagon expedition to California—an event that would* *change the history of California and the Napa Valley forever.*

* *Two other prominent mountain men eventually followed in the footsteps of George Yount and left the life of trapping and trading in the wilderness for a more sedentary life in the Napa Valley. **Julian Pope**, for whom Pope Valley is named, was born in Kentucky, and he came to Mexican territory as a hunter and trapper. In 1830, he went to San Diego to purchase supplies and was arrested for being in Mexico illegally. He was imprisoned for about a year when the captain of an American merchant ship which had entered the port heard of Pope's plight and prevailed upon the Mexican officials to release him. He ultimately obtained a land grant in 1841, naming the property "Rancho Locallome" and brought his family to live there in an adobe house. Pope eventually planted mission grapes on his property in Pope Valley. Injury was a constant danger in the isolated Napa Valley of that time. Only a few years after settling on his rancho in Pope Valley, Julian Pope was hurt in a farming accident and, with no medical help available, he died.*

James Clyman

* ***James Clyman**, a legendary mountain man, and the "plastic surgeon" who stitched Jedediah Smith back together after a bear*

attack, arrived in the Napa Valley in 1846, just after having warned the Sierra-bound Donner Party against taking the treacherous Hastings Cutoff. He lived in the valley until 1881, and the house he built still stands on Redwood Road in the city of Napa, and he is buried in Tulucay Cemetery. Clyman is probably most famous for his "Journal of a Mountain Man" which chronicles his adventures as a trapper and later in the Napa Valley. Although he lived and farmed in the Napa Valley for 35 years, there is no record of him growing grapes on his relatively small property in the south of the Napa Valley.

Chapter IV

Wine in the Napa Valley Early in the American Era

Because of the liberalized policies concerning trade, immigration, and land use in the early part of the 27-year Mexican period in California, a small but often enterprising group of rugged individualists (all of them males) came to California from the U.S. and other parts of the world. They usually came to hunt or trade and usually were not necessarily planning to stay in California. But some of them did stay, and at least two of them, George Yount and William Wolfskill, are now recognized as pioneers and founders of the California wine industry.

For at least two reasons, a true wine industry did not develop in California or the Napa Valley during the Mexican era. First, the small size of the population of California prevented it. (There were only about 10,000 non-indigenous people in California at the end of the Mexican period—2,000 of them immigrants, mostly from the U.S.) Second, the extremely large size of the parcels of land granted by the government to a select group of native-born Mexican citizens and immigrants that became Mexican citizens did not lend itself to the "intensive agriculture" needed to foment a wine industry.

Early Napa Valley Residents Help Usher in the American Era

In 1841, a different kind of immigrant began to arrive in California, coming overland from the United States. This happened in great part because of the influence of Joseph Chiles, an early Napan who would eventually settle in Chiles Valley and become a pioneer grape grower of the Napa Valley. These people were settlers who came to California in large groups in wagon trains with women and children, tools, books, and all of the personal belongings they could carry. They came to California to stay! A great many of these people ended up settling in the Napa Valley, and some of them, more by an accident of history than anything else, would become the agents that changed California from the Mexican to the American era. That change would provide the environment needed to create a true wine industry in the Napa Valley beginning in the middle of the 19th century.

Today, very few people who live in the Napa Valley realize that, to a very large extent, this all took place largely because of Napa Valley residents. The first wagon train to attempt to cross the Sierra Nevada and come to California was the Bidwell-Bartleson Party in 1841. One of its members, and a guide for the party, was Joseph Chiles. When the party arrived at its destination at a *rancho* near Mount Diablo, the members dispersed to various locations in Northern California.

Chiles traveled throughout the northern part of California and came to the Napa Valley to stay with George Yount, whom he had known while both lived in Missouri. To show what a rugged individualist Chiles was, he stayed only long enough to scout out a piece of land he would like to have for himself. He then proceeded to cross the Sierra Nevada, again heading east, returning to Missouri after promising Yount that he would try to bring Yount's family with him when he returned to California. In Missouri, he gathered another group of settlers, including two of George Yount's daughters and the husband of one of the Yount women, and in April of 1842, left for California and came back to the Napa Valley with his entire party.

From then on through the rest of the Mexican period, settlers in wagon trains began making their way over the Sierra Nevada and into California without the permission of the Mexican government. Then in 1846, a large wagon train called the Grigsby-Ide Party arrived in Northern California, and for the Mexican authorities, that seemed to be the straw that broke the camel's back. The Mexicans threatened to send the party back over the mountains after the snowmelt, but having already suffered through a particularly grueling trip getting to California, some of them plotted an insurrection against the Mexicans.

A group, made up mostly of Grigsby-Ide Party immigrants, set out from Sutter's Fort to Sonoma to arrest Mariano Vallejo and declare California an independent country. The Napa Valley contained one of the largest populations of American immigrants living in Mexican California at the time (some of them from the Grigsby-Ide Party who had drifted down to the Napa Valley from Sutter's Fort), and so the insurrectionist made a point to come through the valley on their way to Sonoma to recruit American settlers to join their revolt. There are several accounts of the specific people and numbers of people involved in the Bear Flag Revolt, as this insurrection came to be known. But probably at least 20 of the 33 men who captured the Mexican governor, Vallejo, in Sonoma during the Bear Flag Revolt were from the Napa Valley—that's over 60 percent!

The "Bear Flaggers," as the insurrectionists from the Sacramento and Napa Valleys eventually came to be known did go to Sonoma and capture General Vallejo. They raised the flag of the Bear Flag Republic and declared California to be an independent country. Then, less than a month later, the Bear Flag Republic was abolished by its own founders and the flag of the United States was raised over Sonoma, and the U.S. laid claim to California. Many of the original insurrectionists from the Napa Valley were sworn in at Sonoma as United States Army soldiers and eventually helped to defeat the Mexicans and make California a territory of the United States in 1848. So it was that a group of people who lived in the Napa Valley were in large part responsible for bringing California into the American era, where wine could thrive in the valley.

American Era Sets Stage for Napa Valley Wine Industry

<u>Land:</u> What changed for the Napa Valley wine as a result of the introduction of the American period? First, American lawmakers tended to favor settlement on smaller parcels of land, which were more suitable for intensive agriculture, rather than the large *ranchos* of the Mexican era. The United States government viewed land ownership and land distribution quite differently than did the Mexicans before them. The whole history of American immigration westward reflects the American philosophy, which required that land be distributed much more equally than it was in Mexico's California. The huge land grants of the Mexican era ran counter to the populist tradition in the United States. All through the Midwest during the period prior to the annexation of California, the land was broken into small farms because of a conscious effort on the part of United States government to provide small parcels of land to an ever-increasing and expanding American population. The same pattern prevailed in California after the annexation. Although the U.S. courts sometimes upheld the legality of the large Mexican land grants, more and more those grants not only came under legal attack, but also *de facto* attack by new settlers. Especially after gold was discovered in 1848, the settlers began squatting on the large land grant properties; they purchased small, subdivided parcels or in other ways set about breaking up the large *ranchos*. This applied not only to the *ranchos* owned by the Mexican *Californios,* but also those owned by the early bird Americans like George Yount, who managed to get large parcels of land before the American annexation of California.

The transition in the valley from the *ranchero* of the Mexican era to what noted California historian Kevin Starr has called "the intensive farmer" under American rule sometimes resulted in stress and conflict. "The new immigrants from the east worked to change (the) … landscape. By the time that John Russell Bartlett traversed the Napa Valley as a commissioner with United States and Mexican Boundary Commission in the 1850s, the valley had changed. He stated in his personal narrative that the larger portion of the Napa Valley was still in the state in which nature had left it, but it had all been taken up by recent settlers, and was fast being brought into cultivation … land in the Napa Valley for the overland pioneers was limited though, and by the late 1840s Mexican land grants covered virtually all of the productive soil. Some of the new settlers bought land, and some performed services in exchange for a parcel. Others became squatters."[5] The inevitable result of the increased migration of Americans after the fall of the Mexican government was the subdivision of the valley land into smaller and smaller parcels.

The event that occurred shortly after California became a territory of the United States that had a huge impact on land ownership patterns was the Gold Rush. Squatting on land became a way of life during the Gold Rush, as tens of thousands of immigrants poured into the territory searching for gold in a relatively small area and often later moving to places like the Napa Valley located near the goldfields. Land ownership rights suffered a heavy blow with all of these gold-hungry people entering California. John Sutter lost almost all of his land to squatters during the Gold Rush and spent the latter part of his life in Washington, D.C., trying to reclaim what he had lost. Land squatting and the prevailing policies of the American government were eventually successful in breaking up the large landholdings forever, including those in the Napa Valley. "…As gold fever subsided, squatters settled everywhere, and the breakup of the large *ranchos* escalated. The treaty that ended the Mexican War had guaranteed Californians their liberty and property, but the Land Act of 1851 required all Californians to prove the validly of their land grants. The long, costly process to prove title deprived many landowners of their holdings."[6]

The law stated that land claims dating back to the Mexican era were guaranteed, so long as the land claimed did not exceed 160 acres. Another author described the impact of the Land Act this way:

> Squatters on the huge land grants would thus be guaranteed the right to possess land upon which they could keep a toehold, as in the children's game King of the Mountain. Absentee owners and people who obtained land from them could find their resources drained away in legal expenses trying to defend themselves from intruders.[7]

The impact of this in the Napa Valley was significant.

> Of the original Mexican land grants from Mariano Vallejo, Leese's Huichica, Salvador Vallejo's Yajome, Higuera's Entre Napa, and Yount's Caymus were successfully carved up almost completely by squatters, and the other Mexican land grants eventually succumbed as well. Land ownership became a source of major conflict during this period, and caused tensions to mount between the recent American immigrants and the Mexican grant-holders, California had become a neglected Mexican province.[8]

Certainly the best examples of the impact of the new land policies of the U.S. government are the two most important people in the early history of the Napa Valley prior to the American era: George Yount and Mariano Vallejo. *The History of Napa and Lake Counties*, published in 1881, noted how the transformation of land ownership from the Mexican to the American eras in Napa affected Yount, the valley's first pioneer.

> By now we know well the story of George Yount and his 12,000-acre Caymus rancho. As civilization advanced, his fights with the grizzlies and wild Indians became less and less frequent, but new and more formidable enemies appeared in the land commissioners, squatters, and lawyers. Mr. Yount's history, in this respect, is but a repetition of that of almost every

one of the early settlers in the country. The land, which their own daring and courage rescued from the grizzly and wild Indian, they had to contend for in our courts of law. This is not as it should be. They are all men well advanced in years: their thin locks are white with the frost of many winters. They have played a noble part in the history of our County, and it ill becomes our government to allow them to dwell in anxiety, now.[9]

A similar fate befell Yount's Mexican benefactor Mariano Vallejo, the owner of the largest Northern California rancho of them all. Ellen Lambert Wood, author of a biography of George Yount tells us that:

> In 1851 the government of the United States dealt a fatal blow to General Vallejo, the man who had urged that California come under its protection. The land act of that year threw the validity of titles into confusion, for by it all claims were declared forfeit unless the grantee appeared before the Board of Land Commissioners with proof of ownership. Twelve years later Congress by special act permitted holders of Vallejo's land to buy it at $1.25 per acre. Today nothing remains of his great rancho excepting the home near Sonoma, where his surviving daughter, a most charming woman, lives. At her death it will become the property of the state, and thus will the memory of General Vallejo be preserved.[10]

While this was all obviously disastrous for the land grant holders from the early era, the U.S. government policy concerning the land grants issued during the Mexican period is crucial in explaining how viticulture eventually developed in the Napa Valley. Virtually all of the large landholdings that were the result of Mexican land grants were fairly rapidly broken up early in the American era into smaller parcels that were better suited to intensive farming. However it was done, the United States government was supportive of the subdivision of these vast landholdings into smaller parcels. This was done not only to counter the development of an aristocracy in California, but also to stimulate migration after California became a state. As it turned out, land ownership policies of the

United States also set the stage for the development of viticulture in the Napa Valley.

With the onset of the American era in the Napa Valley, the size and location of land parcels lent themselves much more to the development of agriculture, and more specifically viticulture, than they did the Mexican period. And as has been suggested, a true commercial viticulture industry could never have evolved in the Napa Valley, or any other part of California, during the Mexican period. American land policies, on the other hand, provided an environment where a true commercial wine industry emerged in the Napa Valley.

Speaking specifically of the Napa Valley landholding patterns in the early days of the American era, author William Heitz noted that:

> It is easy to see why wheat and not cattle should have such a strong position in the local economy when the size of the average Napa farm is considered. Of the 640 farmers in the county, nearly 400 cultivated farms of 500 acres or less. Two dozen farmers held farms between 500 to 1,000 acres in size, and a dozen men owned lands totaling more than 1,000 acres. Individually owned cattle herds required thousands of acres of grazing land, not a few hundred. Napa County clearly was not owned by a few cattle barons, as quickly became the case in many California counties.[11]

And of course, these new patterns of land ownership were to have a huge impact on viticulture in the Napa Valley. While a number of the early pioneers in the Mexican era in the Napa Valley are given credit for being the first "vintner" in the valley, that title rightfully belongs to a Napa Valley resident from the American era—John Patchett, who in May of 1852, "... bought from James W. Brackett a hundred-acre parcel near the junction of the Napa River and Napa Creek. In 1856, after California joined the union, Simpson Thompson had a vineyard of 8,000 vines with thirty or so varieties of grapes."[12] (A similar phenomenon occurred in the Sonoma Valley where, after Mariano Vallejo's huge landholdings had been liquidated, Agoston Haraszthy started the Buena Vista Vineyards, on a much smaller piece of land. He ultimately became the "Father of Viticulture in California.")

John Osborn is one more example of someone from the early American era with a small piece of land who dedicated it to agriculture and viticulture.

> Another man who advanced viticulture in the valley in the 1850s was John Osborn. In 1856, his farm won the first prize for the best farm given by the state agricultural society. That award drew considerable attention to Napa Valley's agricultural resources. ... Osborn Vineyard was then second only to (Simpson) Thompson's in size with 6,000 vines, of which half were foreign varieties. There was no standard spacing of the vines, if he planted 682 the acre over (rather common), he would've had about *ten acres* (emphasis of mine) in all.[13]

Using the same formula, Simpson Thompson in the summer of 1856 founded a vineyard of 8,000 vines that would have been around 12 acres, and John Patchett had 55 acres in the early 1850s.

This diversified ownership of the arable land of the valley by 1860 was one of Napa's early strengths in the American era because it attracted men with an interest in all areas of agriculture, from wheat and orchard farming to viticulture. Farmers could shift their crops readily depending upon weather conditions, or as market prices dictated.

And, indeed, the Napa Valley had a competitive advantage with the surrounding territories in Northern California and in the Central Valley in the creation of "agricultural entrepreneurs." This was because, as historian Kevin Starr points out, "'intensive farmers' showed up in Southern California orchards and vineyards relatively early in the American era, much later in other parts of Northern California, and virtually *not at all* in the Central Valley, which has followed the 'agrobiz' model of massive scale farming from the earliest days of agriculture." Fortunately for the Napa Valley, "intensive farmers" began showing up in the 1850s, and some of them began to cultivate vineyards.

Trade: The acquisition of California by United States brought with it one obvious windfall for the Napa Valley: the potential for free trade with the rest the country. We saw earlier that external trade was forbidden in the Spanish era and extremely limited in the Mexican, but the acquisition of California by the United States opened up almost unlimited domestic and worldwide markets to the valley.

Despite the opening of these new markets, California and the Napa Valley were still too isolated from the rest of the U.S., and so they couldn't take advantage of them. However, the mountain came to Mohammed in 1848. Tens of thousands, followed by hundreds of thousands of people began arriving in California in search of gold. It isn't very well known today, but the Napa Valley was the "breadbasket" of the Gold Rush era. With all those 49ers wandering around the foothills north of the valley, there became an enormous demand for flour. Wheat farming presented a huge opportunity to exploit new markets right in California itself. Many of the residents of the Napa Valley dropped everything and headed for the mines during the Gold Rush, but for those staying behind, the trade in flour became extremely profitable. The Napa Valley, with approximately 35,000 acres under cultivation around the time of the Gold Rush, became the second-largest producer of wheat in California behind the Santa Clara Valley.

In fact, all the way up until 1860 and beyond, Napa was known primarily for its wheat production. In that year, a freelance journalist wrote:

> North of San Pablo Bay and the opening upon it, are three valleys side by side parallel with each other and with the coast. … Each is drained by a creek bearing its own name, and bounded by a steep range of mountains on both sides; and each is rich in wealth different from that of the others. Petaluma has the dairies, Sonoma has the wine, and Napa has wheat.[14]

The Gold Rush was the first stimulus for the earliest wine trade, as well, although the volume was quite small and wine trade on a large-scale did not begin for the Napa Valley until the mid-to-late 1850s.

> The Gold Rush helped introduce another factor in Napa Valley's development. Gold miners and new settlers desired something to drink. Napa Valley (as well as other locations) set about to satisfy this desire with wine production. Still the major crops of the Napa Valley through the 1860s were wheat, apples, pears, horses, and cattle.[15]

As previously noted, George Yount first introduced *Vitis vinifera* into the Napa Valley, but made little, if any, wine from the vines he brought owing to religious beliefs about alcohol or the rigors of his pioneer life in the valley, or both. But even Yount was enticed to produce wine for the thirsty 49ers scrambling for gold in the foothills to the north. However, the wine trade in the Napa Valley really had its beginning *after* Yount's early attempts to sell wine to the thirsty 49ers, when John Patchett "...shipped wine regularly from 1857 and won a great deal more press notice for the valley's wine than the man from Yountville (George Yount)."[16] Patchett is also credited with "the first shipment of wine from Napa County and that took place in 1857. Patchett sent six casks and 600 bottles of wine, probably to San Francisco."[17]

The annexation of California, followed by the Gold Rush, opened small markets to Napa's wine trade, but the larger markets for wine would not emerge until later. In fact, it was tough sledding in the very early days of winemaking in the Napa Valley.

> Eastern Americans, during much of the 19th century, developed a wine snobbery against so-called 'Native Wines' that made it difficult, almost impossible, to sell Napa Valley or California wine in many of the first-class hotels and restaurants. Wine from eastern states such as New York or Ohio fared even less well, it should be quickly noted; it was the French label that was preferred on the wine bottle.[18]

So, while the trade opportunities that came with the American era in California combined with new land distribution policies to make the birth of the wine industry in the Napa Valley possible, these very early days were still quite difficult for the people who were the first to try their hand at the wine business in the valley. George Crane was a very early pioneer in seeking to create a true wine industry in the Napa Valley, and his experience illustrates how tough it was to get the wine trade started. Author William Heintz notes:

> In the late 1860s he (Crane) shipped several thousand gallons of red and white to New York City and journeyed there himself to supervise its sale. He apparently could not find a dealer who would even purchase one barrel of his wine, the market being taken completely by imported, mainly French wine. The problem was one he had not anticipated: eastern American wines from native grapes (rough, foxy were commonly used adjectives) were of a far different taste than French wine. It was assumed by eastern dealers that California wines would taste the same. The few newspaper stories already published on the high quality of California wine had not been able to open the doors of New York wine merchants.[19]

The earliest trade opportunities for the Napa Valley wine business to come during the American era came from within California itself, especially from San Francisco. With the discovery of gold came a robust market for the wine of the Napa Valley just a short distance to the southwest in the booming metropolis of San Francisco. By the beginning of 1850, the population of California was estimated at 107,000 people. Thousands of gold seekers had crossed the mountains into the Gold Country, and thousands came by sea as well, usually landing in San Francisco. This growing population was made up of people from all over the world, many of whom came from countries where wine was an essential part of life, and who significantly increased the market for California wine as time went by.

> By the onset of the Civil War, because of the unquenchable thirst of the diversified group of immigrants who ended up

settling in San Francisco, the Napa Valley began to nurture a healthy local wine market focused, of course, in booming San Francisco.[20]

Even though the American era opened trade possibilities that launched the wine business in the Napa Valley, it took the advance of the transcontinental railroad to truly open the American market for wine outside of California. The impact of the transcontinental railroad began to be felt in the early 1870s.

> ...Napa Valley wine was shipped in carload lots to the East as early as 1873, via the new transcontinental railroad. ... (Napa vintners) had pooled resources and sent a carload of wine to the Detroit, Michigan. This may have been the first large-scale shipping of wine from the valley to the eastern states.[21]

As the market for Napa Valley wine gradually expanded, vintners tried to exploit any market they could, and opportunities arose from unanticipated places.

> Oddly enough, the Civil War, fought thousands of miles away, had a strong effect on the wine industry. Because of the interruptions in shipping many goods manufactured in the East were unable to reach California and other western destinations; thriving home industries began to meet just about every consumer need. French wines, which had a strong foothold in San Francisco restaurants became unavailable, and California vintners were delighted with the new demand for 'native wines'.[22]

The early success during the Gold Rush and the Civil War fed upon itself, and as time passed, vintners in the Napa Valley and surrounding viticulture areas began to get a little more sophisticated about marketing and developing the Napa Valley wine trade. After the Civil War, organizations designed to help vintners to market as well as produce their vines were established, including the Grape Growers Association of Sonoma, Napa, and Solano Counties; The California Vine Growers and Wine Brandy Manufacturers Association; and the Helena Viticultural Club.

As businessmen became involved in the wine industry, investors began to apply business principles to producing and merchandising their products. A marketing group, the Napa Valley Wine Company, formed with the express purpose of packaging and selling certain Napa Valley wine to consumers outside the state. ... And (the members) established branch offices in New York and St. Louis. A similar but larger organization, the California Wine Association formed in 1894 around the NVWC consolidating it with Greystone and the Uncle Sam Winery. Some vintners may have resented the select joining the forces, but the result was a greater market reach and more consistent quality in the wine being offered.[23]

The Napa Viticultural Society was organized in May of 1881 along the lines of the St. Helena Viticultural Society and provided information and data for vintners, while promoting their products in California and across the country to the extent they could.

So, while it took some time for a true wine industry to develop in the Napa Valley, it is pretty obvious that the onset of the American era in California opened great opportunities for trade. From virtually no wine trade in the Mexican era, the wine industry had been launched in the Napa Valley and had enough momentum to provide a steady demand for Napa wines and to attract new vintners (primarily from Europe) by the 1860s.

Immigration: After the successful Bear Flag Revolt of 1846, immigration into the Napa Valley and other parts of the California continued, but at a slow pace. Then, in the incredible year of 1848, a "perfect storm" hit and changed the character of the Napa Valley forever.

This rare combination of circumstances resulted from U.S. policy regarding land use (previously discussed), and two forces influencing immigration that came together in a most fortuitous way for the Napa Valley. The first factor influencing immigration was the Gold Rush, which resulted in hundreds of thousands of people streaming into California by land and sea, which increased

California's population almost exponentially. Prior to the discovery of gold at Sutter's Mill in 1848, virtually the only non-Mexican immigrants to California were the more or less homogenous groups of people from the immigrant parties. They came primarily from Missouri and adjoining U.S. frontier states, and they were more likely than not from what might be called society's fringe groups. They were people with agrarian backgrounds from the American frontier who were fleeing the climate, disease, and socioeconomic conditions to go to a completely unknown territory and a completely unknown fate.

The Gold Rush changed all that. The people (mostly men) who came to the gold fields during the California Gold Rush were a disparate group with many different talents and skills, and they were almost by definition entrepreneurial spirits. A newspaper noted at the time, "All classes of our citizens seem to be under the influence of this extraordinary mania which exceeds everything in the history of commercial adventure."[24]

They came from around Cape Horn, across the Isthmus of Panama, and by way of the major overland routes to California, and they came in huge numbers.

> In 1849, scores of ships carried at least 17,000 gold seekers. From the United States westward trails were crowded with more than 42,000 49ers, while another 25,000 reached California by sea. In April of 1850, the overwhelmed harbormaster at San Francisco estimated the number who had landed during the previous twelve months at over 62,000, from ports around the globe. For years thereafter, gold seekers by the hard-to-count thousands pushed ashore at California suddenly famous city.[25]

As far as the overland crossings were concerned, "At least 32,000 made their way in 1849, probably 44,018 in 1850, and in 1851 an astonishing crest of 50,000."[26] As might be imagined, an influx of hundreds of thousands of people arriving in California in a matter of just a few years dramatically changed the nature of the place and had a huge impact on the development of the Napa Valley as well.

Many of these people planned to come to California, stay only a short while and then return to their homes with their pockets full of gold. However, many of them stayed and, not only that, sent for their families and friends to join them. Many eventually migrated to metropolitan centers like San Francisco or the agricultural areas in Northern California, and some became consumers of Napa Valley wine. Some of them settled in the Napa Valley itself, increasing the pool of workers and landowners in the valley. And the valley, thanks to the onset of the American era, was now socially and politically ready to accept people who had the wherewithal to buy the *small* plots of land that were now available, or who wanted to become city folk and settle in the slowly growing city of Napa.

All of a sudden, the Napa Valley was not just a little valley with a tiny population composed of the pioneers and settlers as it was in very earliest days of immigration. At first, the new immigrants to the valley focused on wheat farming to supply flour to the miners in the fields just north of the valley. But viticulture would continue to grow in importance, and the Napa Valley would go from having virtually no true vineyards before the Gold Rush to having 433 vineyards in 1881. Immigration resulting from the Gold Rush at first turned the sleepy Napa Valley into the "breadbasket" of California and then fairly rapidly into a center of California wine production.

The other component of the "perfect storm" of immigration to California in general, and the Napa Valley in particular in 1848, was the tremendous turmoil that occurred throughout Europe that year, prompting many of the most dissatisfied and oft times most highly talented members of Europe's middle class to seek opportunities elsewhere. Many of them immigrated to the United States in order to avoid political persecution or to avoid living under regimes they found to be repressive. The Gold Rush provided the perfect rationale for many of these people to flee their native lands and come to California.

Although nobody would have imagined it at the time, the European revolutions in 1848 were to have a huge impact on the development of the Napa Valley wine industry. When revolutions erupted throughout Europe in 1848, Prague, Paris, Naples, and Berlin were beset by radicals who were interested in overthrowing the conservative establishments of Europe. Every one of the revolts failed, and resulted in authoritarian political regimes coming to power throughout Europe.

The revolutions of 1848 were brought on by "bourgeois liberals" who sought to defend the privileges they had acquired as a result of the French Revolution and the Napoleonic Empire, and which were being eroded by the restored monarchies. In France, the struggle was about property ownership qualifications. In Prussia, it was about the abolition of serfdom and the agrarian reform. In Germany, the conservative ruling class met the outbreaks that led the bourgeoisie to seek radical political reforms with ironfisted resistance.

Here is how Gold Rush historian J. S. Holliday describes the impact on California of the European turmoil of 1848:

> Insurrections, abdications, wars of independence, and wars of dynastic restoration had released chaos of rioting street fighting in Paris (12,000 killed, 25,000 arrested in June 1848), demonstrations in Vienna and Prague, strikes in Berlin. Amidst such tumult, the news from California offered compelling reasons to embrace an old idea: immigration to the New World. In 1849 would-be miners boarded hundreds of ships that carried them 14,000 miles around Cape Horn to San Francisco, distant gateway to a new life.[27]

As a consequence of the problems in Europe in the mid-1800s, a *qualitative* change took place in the immigrants who came to California and the Napa Valley. Instead of just the raw pioneers and settlers from the American frontier populating the Napa Valley, skilled, well-educated, and well-to-do immigrants from European countries steeped in the tradition of wine and winemaking began to make their homes in the Napa Valley. They were enterprising people of means who could identify *terroir* appropriate for the cultivation of vines for the making of wine. As historian J. S. Holliday tells us:

> Less fertile land in the valley, found to be unsuited to orchards and grains, proved invaluable for vines. Many impressed with the valley came with wine on their minds, and set out to plant the available land. … Thanks to the colorful Count Haraszthy [who actually settled in the Sonoma Valley but who fits perfectly the profile of the Europeans we're talking about] European varieties were introduced about 1860.[28]

Napa Historian Lin Weber points out:

> Many Germans and French people migrated to the Napa Valley in the second half of the 19th century. On the whole they came not as laborers but as entrepreneurs who saw something in the valley that resembled their homeland. Following the Civil War and during the early 1870s, several hundred European immigrants settled here and many started wineries.[29]

Another historian noted that:

> All but five of the forty-nine winemakers (in Napa) in 1879 were men of wealth, from European winemaking backgrounds.[30]

So, thanks to the huge influx of immigrants into California from the United States and all over the world who arrived seeking riches during the Gold Rush, and thanks also to the arrival of a subset of immigrants from Europe into the Napa Valley who were perfectly suited to pursue serious viticulture and oenology, a real wine culture and wine industry was set to emerge in the Napa Valley. It is time to take a look at these immigrants to the valley, especially those "refugees" from Europe's revolutions of 1848, and see what kind of people they were and what they accomplished after they arrived.

People: Because the residents of the Napa Valley played such an important role in launching the Bear Flag Revolt, which began the American era in California, they were, to a great degree, masters of their own destiny. Recall that the majority of the men who fought on the rebels' side in the Bear Flag Revolt were from the Napa Valley, and that many went on to fight with the California Battalion which helped to finalize the transfer of sovereignty in California from the Mexicans to the Americans. The advent of the American era resulted in a major structural conversion of land use in the Napa Valley. The valley went from being the economically inefficient home to a small number of landowners with huge tracts of mostly unused land to an area that not only offered the natural resources required, but also a landownership structure well suited to viticulture. Add to this the potential for trading wine within California, the rest of the U.S., and the outside world made possible by the new American trade policies. Finally, add the potential for immigrants with the skills required for great grape growing and winemaking to come to the Napa Valley, which was now a part of the United States, and you now have a valley that is a candidate to be a significant wine-producing region of the world.

But it was the individual unique *people* who came to the Napa Valley after it became a part of the U.S. that made it all happen. All of the other natural resources—the *terroir* required for growing grapes can be there, and the government policies concerning land ownership, trade and immigration can be put in place, as happened when the U.S. took control of California and the Napa Valley, but if people with the right backgrounds, training, skills, and work ethic are not there, all of the great potential will never be realized. As it turned out, the Napa Valley was fortunate enough in the early years of the American era to attract the right people, who would develop the wine industry and the wine culture in the valley. There are five of these people—Charles Krug, Jacob Schram, Jacob and Frederick Beringer, and Gustave Niebaum—who made the greatest contribution and left the greatest legacy to the valley, and they will be the focus of attention in the next chapter. But there are also some other people who contributed to the development of the wine industry and culture of the Napa Valley who deserve attention.

Truly dedicated commercial viticulture and winemaking did not come to the Napa Valley until the arrival of Charles Krug in 1858, but the earlier experimentation and small-scale production of wine proved that viticulture was possible there. It also created the beginnings of a wine industry infrastructure, and this eventually attracted true winemaking entrepreneurs. We saw that George Yount not only planted the first *Vitis vinifera* grapes in the Napa Valley but also engaged in small-scale wine commerce when the 49ers arrived during the Gold Rush. The Napa Valley landowner already mentioned as the first to have a true vineyard was John Patchett, an Englishman who came to California for the Gold Rush at the fairly advanced age of more than 50 years. Patchett made some money in mining and eventually came to the Napa Valley to find land to farm. He bought a 100-acre parcel and became "the first one to plant a vineyard of any consequence for any other purpose than for grapes for table use."[31] He only produced wine from mission grapes and had a modest operation at best. In 1859, Patchett constructed a stone cellar for storing his wines, and he is also credited with being the first to ship wine from Napa County when, in 1857, he sent a shipment to San Francisco. Consequently, Patchett should probably be credited as the first to sell wine commercially, even though George Yount did sell some during the Gold Rush.

Patchett was joined by early grape-growing pioneers like John Osborn and Simpson Thompson, who grew grapes and made and sold wine, although they did not focus exclusively on wine production. Patchett also deserves recognition as being a man who first invited Charles Krug to the Napa Valley from his home in the Sonoma Valley to make wine from the grapes he had planted on his property. After Krug left to marry Edward Bale's daughter, Caroline, and began growing his own grapes on the property that was his wife's dowry, Patchett brought in Henry A. Pellet, who continued Krug's work at Patchett's winery and also went on to make wine for Dr. George Belden Crane. Crane was an enlightened early grape grower who recognized the potential for growing numerous great varietals in the Napa Valley and who was one of the first to produce large volumes of wine in the 1860s.

For his part, Pellet eventually left Crane and went on to become a partner in one of the other early large wineries in the valley. Other early residents of the Napa Valley got involved with wine as well. For example, Sam Brannan, who led an early settler party of Mormons to California and went on to promote a resort in what is now Calistoga, planted vines on a farm he acquired in the Napa Valley in 1857. William Thompson, who like Pellet made money in the goldfields, bought property in the Napa Valley, where his brother Simpson joined him in 1852. They establish some orchards that gained some local notoriety, and they recognized the potential for grapevines on their land, where they eventually planted several varietals.

All of these men are examples of people who, because of the new land, trading, and immigration policies of the American era, came to the Napa Valley and each in his own way saw the potential for wine. While each of these men contributed to the early history of wine in the Napa Valley, one among them, Charles Krug, was a true visionary. He, along with four other men who followed him, would leave the legacy of the Napa Valley wine culture that is the subject of the next chapter of this book.

Chapter IV Appendix:

People, Places, and Things at the End of the Mexican Period and During the Early American Period

U.S. Immigrant Settlers

The mountain men, like those from the Wolfskill Party, helped to open California, which, except for visits to its coast by an occasional rogue foreign vessel, had been completely isolated from the outside world save weak ties to central Mexico. Mountain men trapped and traded in California and some, like George Yount, settled in California. In Yount's case, he even planted vineyards in what would become one of the greatest wine regions of the world. Others, like Antoine Robidoux, would return to the U.S. frontier and encourage other people—not necessarily mountain men or frontiersmen—to travel to California. In addition to Robidoux, there were two other sources of material on California that began to inspire more ordinary people to try to go to California. One of them was the "Report of an Exploring Expedition to the Rocky Mountains in the Year 1842 and to Oregon & North California in the Years 1843-44" by John Fremont, who, guided by Kit Carson of the Wolfskill Party, came to California twice in the early 1840s. His report to the government was published and widely circulated in the

U.S. The other was a group of letters sent from California by a Harvard-educated mountain man named John Marsh.

John Marsh

• ***John Marsh*** *graduated from Harvard College in 1823, where he studied medicine, although he did not complete his degree. He came to California across the mountains by way of the Santa Fe Trail and ended up in Los Angeles, where he practiced medicine— and did so quite well it is said—without a medical degree. He then went north and eventually became the owner of Rancho Los Medanos in 1838. It lay at the foot of Mt. Diablo near present-day Antioch. Apropos of the Californio/rancho lifestyle and the economy of California at the time, Marsh was paid for his medical services in the currency of the California rancho—hides and tallow! Marsh greatly enjoyed his life in California and began a letter-writing campaign extolling the virtues of the land. He had an ulterior motive, however, because he thought he would have a better future if more people came from the U.S. He also had hopes that the United States would eventually annex California.*

- *Somehow or other, his letters about California reached the newspapers of Missouri in the early 1840s and set off a flurry of interest in California. It was largely because of the writings of John Marsh and the town hall speech given by Antoine Robidoux that John Bidwell, the leader of the Bidwell-Bartleson Party—the first group of settlers to cross the Sierra successfully—made the decision to come to California. In fact, after arriving in California, they went directly to Marsh's house, not knowing where else to go.*

John Bidwell

- *John Bidwell led the Bidwell-Bartleson Party in 1841, the first emigrant wagon train to travel what came to be called the Oregon-California Trail. This wagon train became symbolic to the Americans they left behind because it was the first party of settlers to actually make it to California. Although it was the first to arrive, the party had to abandon its wagons in what is now Nevada. The first party to cross the Sierra Nevada Mountains with its wagons was the Stevens-Murphy-Townsend Party of 1844. Many people in Missouri and elsewhere were later stimulated to go to California themselves, increasing the number of American settlers in the Mexican territory. The Bidwell-Bartleson Party was also important for the Napa Valley because it brought the valley its first settler from an immigrant party, Joseph Chiles.*

• *The Bidwell-Bartleson Party of 32 men, one woman, and a child left Sapling Grove, Missouri on May 9, 1841 and arrived in California at the home of John Marsh six months later. John Bidwell was one of the larger-than-life figures in the story of American migration to California. After leaving Marsh's house, Bidwell went to work for John Sutter at Sutter's Fort until 1844, when he left to look for gold in the southern part of the state. He then went back to Sutter's Fort and continued to work there, and was one of the men from Sutter's who participated in the Bear Flag Revolt. He was back working as Sutter's "General Businessman" when John Marshall first discovered gold at Sutter's Mill in 1848. Bidwell was one of the few people from the settler parties to strike it rich in the Gold Rush by finding a large deposit of gold at Bidwell's Bar on the Feather River in July of that year.*

Joseph Chiles

• ***Joseph Chiles***, *a member of the Bidwell-Bartleson Party, was an accomplished frontiersman who assisted in guiding the aggregation to California. After arriving at Marsh's home, Chiles made several stops around Northern California. He visited American settlers, General Mariano Vallejo, and eventually George Yount, whom he had known in Missouri. Chiles explored the area around the Napa Valley and decided he wanted to obtain a land grant for what is now* *known as Chiles Valley. After stopping off at Sutter's Fort, he immediately returned to Missouri to begin signing up people to go into another wagon train to California. Included in the group were two of George Yount's daughters and his son-in-law. Eventually, after the group merged with another party heading west, there were over 50 people in total. Chiles signed up Joseph Walker, a noted mountain man, to help guide the party, and this time the wagons did make it across the Sierra and ended up in the Napa Valley. Many of these people ended up settling in the valley, making it one of the largest settlements of Americans in Mexican California.*

John Sutter

• *John Sutter is the most famous of the very early California pioneers because he was given a land grant by the Mexican government that would dramatically change the history of California. Not only was gold discovered on his property, setting off the Gold Rush of 1848, but he also played a big part in the history of California and the history of the Napa Valley long before the Gold Rush began. Almost every important event in the area north of the San Francisco Bay in the 1840s involved John Sutter in some way or another. His "empire," which he called New Helvetia, served as a waypoint for almost all the pioneers who came to California over the Sierra Nevada Mountains.*

- *After only a few weeks at John Marsh's house, the pioneers of the Bidwell-Bartleson Party left. Marsh was a great promoter of California, and the members of the party took his offer of hospitality to heart. But when 34 bedraggled souls actually took him up on coming to California and showed up at his house—starving and minus almost all of their possessions—he was beside himself. He allowed them to stay on his property, but when they ate his prized oxen, Marsh lost his temper and evicted his guests. Most of them then went to Sutter's Fort. Sutter was a Swiss immigrant to the U.S. who left his family in the Old World and, after arriving in America, went west to Missouri, where he worked as an innkeeper and merchant for several years. Because his land was located at the conjunction of the American and Sacramento Rivers near the western foothills of the Sierra Nevada, where so many pioneers and settlers descended into California by land, it is curious that John Sutter actually arrived in California by ship. In reality, he should probably be categorized as a mountain man. In 1838, he joined a fur trapping party and for many years was a trapper and roamed the frontier like other mountain men. Ultimately, his trapping party went north and ended up in Fort Vancouver. Unable to leave immediately for California, Sutter sailed on a trading ship for the Sandwich Islands (Hawaiian Islands). He landed in Honolulu, and from there he sailed to Sitka, Alaska, and finally to Yerba Buena (later named San Francisco). Sutter then met with Mexican governor, Alvarado, in Monterey to discuss settling in California.*

- *After traveling by boat up the Sacramento River and exploring the surrounding land, he received a land grant for a very large parcel of land in the western foothills of the Sierra. Of course, part of the land Sutter settled on was the site where gold was first discovered. However, it was as a settler that John Sutter first had a huge impact on California and on the Napa Valley—long before the Gold Rush. Sutter's Fort provided a haven for a seemingly endless number of pioneers and settlers, with quite a few of them eventually settling in the Napa Valley. Sutter also signed many bonds of good behavior, assuring the Mexican government of the trustworthiness of most of the*

U.S. settlers coming over the Sierra Mountains. The group of settlers that would carry out the Bear Flag Revolt began their march from around Sutter's Fort and came down through the Napa Valley, where many of the Valley residents became insurrectionists and joined the revolution. John Sutter was in the thick of the action in California throughout the 1840s. Unfortunately, he spent the latter years of his life rather tragically in Washington, D.C. trying to recover the land and empire he had worked so hard to build but had ironically lost to immigrant squatters during the Gold Rush.

John Grigsby and William Ide

Overland Immigration to California 1841-46

1841	34
1842	---
1843	38
1844	53
1845	260
1846	1,500

From John Sutter: a Life on the North American Frontier by Albert L. Hurtado (Norman: U. of Oklahoma Press, 2006), p.90 Based on John D. Unruh, Jr. The Plains Across: The Overland Immigrants and the Trans-Mississippi West, 1840-60 (Urban: University of Illinois Press, 1979) p.119

• ***The Grigsby-Ide Party*** *arrived at Sutter's Fort in 1846, when, as the table opposite shows, the rate of immigration from the U.S. to California (almost all of it by way of Sutter's Fort) really became noticeably greater. The Grigsby-Ide Party was important to California and the Napa Valley because it not only brought another large group of settlers, but its arrival changed the equation for the Mexicans. They now had concerns about what had become thousands of Americans streaming into California each year. This situation was to change things forever for California and for the Napa Valley because the negative reaction of the Mexicans to the arrival of the Grigsby-Ide Party subsequently resulted in the revolt which ultimately ushered in the American era in California. The people in this party endured the hardships of coming to California, but after their arrival, they soon began to feel as if those dreams might be snatched from them. The Mexicans threatened to force the party back out of California as soon as spring arrived.*

• *Faced with this grim possibility, a small group of members of the Grigsby-Ide Party, along with a few other men who had been in California before the party arrived, decided to act preemptively. They took up arms and traveled by horseback from where they were camped near Sutter's Fort, down through the Napa Valley to pick up other recruits. Their forces "swelling" to 33 men (possibly as many as 22 of them from the Napa Valley), they proceeded to Sonoma, the home of Mariano Vallejo. As the administrator of the territory north of San Francisco, he had generously provided land grants in the past to the earlier arrivals from America. Many members of this band of immigrants from the U.S., the "Bear Flaggers," had just arrived in California with the Grigsby-Ide Party. They would capture Vallejo and successfully carry off the Bear Flag Revolt with only two casualties on either side.*

• *The Mexican period that these immigrants helped bring to an end saw the discovery and settlement of the Napa Valley and the introduction of mission varietal vines. But as far as is known, no production of wine. In the early American period, three forces caused the huge land grant properties to be broken up: the introduction of new land use laws; an influx of squatters who came with the Gold Rush; and the opening of a regional market for wine, spawned by the Gold Rush. The huge land grant properties in the Napa Valley were gradually broken up, and a small wine industry was established by men like* **John Patchett, John Osborn** *and* **Simpson Thompson***, the earliest pioneers of wine in the Napa Valley.*

Chapter V

The Establishment of the Wine Industry and Wine Culture of the Napa Valley in the American Era

The "perfect storm" that dramatically changed the Napa Valley from wilderness to wine country began in 1848. It would not only change the character of the valley forever, it would ultimately define its wine culture and the development of a wine industry in the early history of the valley in the American era. The three major forces making up the Napa Valley perfect storm in 1848 were: American land use laws and customs, the Gold Rush, and the European Revolutions.

1. American Land Use Laws and Customs Beginning in 1848

The first force contributing to the perfect storm of 1848 was the establishment of American rule and American laws and customs when California became a territory of the United States. All through the Midwest during the period prior to the annexation of California, the land was redistributed as a result of a conscious effort on the part of United States government to provide small parcels of land to an ever-increasing and expanding American population.

Although the U.S. courts sometimes upheld the legality of the large Mexican land grants, more and more those grants came under legal attack. The Land Act of 1851 required all Californians to prove the validly of their land grants. From that point on, the large land grant properties from the Mexican era in the Napa Valley would continue to be broken up into smaller parcels.

2. The Gold Rush of 1848

After gold was discovered in 1848, many of the thousands of gold-seekers found their way into the fertile Napa Valley. Through both squatting and purchasing small, subdivided parcels of land, the new residents began the process of breaking up the large ranchos. According to historians Denzil and Jennie Verado, "...the original Mexican land grants from Mariano Vallejo... (such as) Yount's Caymus were successfully carved up almost completely by squatters, and the other Mexican land grants eventually succumbed as well."[32]

The Gold Rush changed the basic social structure of the Napa Valley too. Prior to the discovery of gold in 1848, virtually the only non-Mexican immigrants to California were the more or less homogenous groups of agrarian people of the immigrant parties coming from the Midwestern frontier of the U.S. After the Gold Rush, people who came to the goldfields during the California Gold Rush were a disparate group from many parts of the U.S. and the world with lots of different talents and skills, and they were almost by definition entrepreneurial spirits. Many of these people eventually settled in the Napa Valley, changing forever the little valley with its tiny population composed of Mexican and foreign pioneers and settlers.

3. The European Revolutions of 1848

The final converging force of the perfect storm of immigration to the Napa Valley beginning in 1848 was a bit of a rouge wave. The year 1848 was the beginning of tremendous political and social turmoil throughout Europe, prompting many of the most dissatisfied and oftentimes most highly talented members of Europe's middle class to seek opportunities elsewhere. Many of them immigrated to the United States in order to avoid political persecution or to avoid living under regimes they found to be repressive. The Gold Rush provided the perfect rationale for many of these people to flee their native lands and come to California.

Although nobody would have imagined it at the time, the European Revolutions of 1848 were to have a huge impact on the development of the Napa Valley wine industry. As a consequence of the problems in Europe beginning in 1848, another type of immigrant became a part of the blend in the Napa Valley. Skilled, well-educated, and well-to-do newcomers from European countries steeped in the tradition of wine and winemaking began to make their homes here.

They were enterprising people of means who could identify *terroir* appropriate for the cultivation of vines for making wine. Often, it took these European immigrants many years to reach the Napa Valley. However, many people from Germany, France, and other wine-loving regions of Europe arrived in the valley after 1848 steeped in the traditions of those regions and with the idea of grape growing and winemaking on their minds.

The Wine Culture of the Napa Valley and the Men Who Defined It

Five men stand out among the special people who arrived from Europe to help launch the wine industry during the "perfect storm" in the Napa Valley. These five men were special because each of them set in motion traditions that define the essence of the wine culture of the Napa Valley all the way up to this very day. There are many early vintners like those mentioned at the end of the previous chapter whose hard work and perseverance helped to establish the wine industry in the valley and who "made a difference" by producing quality wine and by drawing the attention of wine consumers to Napa Valley wines in the very early days. But the five men we are about to discuss each in his own way made a huge contribution to the "Napa Valley wine culture" that is the essence of the Napa Valley.

One of the reasons for studying history (probably the single most important reason) is to learn where we have been and how we got to where we are now. The story of these five extraordinary men from history will tell us much about how the Napa Valley came to be what it now is. The place has its own unique "Napa Valley wine culture" because to wine lovers throughout the world, the Napa Valley is more than just the valley or the wines it produces, it has its own unique place in the world of wine.

As those lucky enough to have visited some of the great wine regions of the world know, each of these regions has its very own unique mix of attributes and each its own unmistakable character or "wine culture." All have rows of grapevines proven over time to thrive in the *terroir* that prevails in the region. They also have the tradition, accumulated knowledge, skilled people, equipment, and buildings, etc. needed to produce their magnificent wines. But the wine culture of each of these regions is a more complex matter because it goes beyond the land or the wine and extends to the "total experience" of the place.

It is not suggested that any of the attributes of the Napa Valley about to be listed are unique to the valley, but rather that the valley combines these qualities in a way that makes it different from the other great wine regions of the world. In a sense, the wine culture of a region is its DNA. Those who have visited Bordeaux for example know that its wines are perhaps the greatest in the world, and the beautiful chateaux nestled among the vineyards represent a wine tradition unparalleled anywhere else in the world. However, for the average tourist in Bordeaux, a visit to the hospitality facilities in the chateaux is often less than a memorable experience. This is because one would not go to Bordeaux hoping to compare the flavors of the number of wine varietals because all of the great chateaux of Bordeaux produce only one or a very small number of wines made from blending just a few grape varietals. In Tuscany, a visitor might expect some great dining experiences and hospitality, but less in the way of different varietals to taste or leading-edge viticulture and oenology techniques to learn about. So each of the great wine regions of the world can be said to have its own distinct wine culture and, it should be added, no wine culture of the world is necessarily better than any other, just different.

It will be left to others to list the qualities that make up the wine culture of other regions, but there are five attributes of the Napa Valley that define its unique wine culture: wine excellence, varietal diversity, innovation, ambience, and hospitality.

1. Wine Excellence: The quality and excellence of the wines can be attributed in part to centuries-old techniques originally developed in Europe and adapted to the special conditions found in the Napa Valley. But in addition, the development of scientific methods and new technologies in both viticulture and oenology have always been welcomed and encouraged. The relationships between the valley and various campuses of the University of California are well known. Countless new advances in growing grapes, fighting disease, implementing sanitation techniques, fermenting, and aging wine, have resulted from Napa Valley wineries serving as seedbeds for research. Of course, this is not to say that other wine regions of the world have not embraced science and technology. But there were times in some of them, especially in Europe, where "Black Magic" passed down through the generations and over the centuries was much more the rule than the scientific method.

2. Varietal Diversity: The vintners of the Napa Valley have, since the very beginning, experimented with numerous varietals to offer to their customers. The most popular varietals may have changed over the years, but most valley wineries usually feature a comparatively large number of varietals, and have introduced their customers to new types of wine or have changed the wine varietals they make in order to serve the current demands of the marketplace. In the Old World wine regions, this is often not the case. Many wine regions in Europe are famous for one or a few varietals and focus exclusively on them. In some places, notably France, the law determines which varietals can be grown in each appellation. An

abiding characteristic of the Napa Valley wine culture of today is the plethora of wine varietals offered, and a willingness on the part of the vintners to change varietals to suit the tastes of wine drinkers.

3. Innovation: While the Napa Valley has now an established tradition of high-quality viticulture and oenology, it has never been reluctant to try new approaches, not only to wine and winemaking but also in providing a satisfying experience for its visitors. Throughout history in the Napa Valley, vintners have grown vines in areas not thought to be sustainable. They have not been afraid to try new rootstocks and clones or experiment with and adopt new techniques for fermenting, storing, and aging wine. In addition, they have displayed beautiful works of art to please the aesthetic tastes of visitors and established wine education programs and special food and wine events. Traditions are revered in the Napa Valley, but not to the extent that they are in some winegrowing regions in the Old World, and certainly not to the exclusion of innovation.

4. Ambience: The Napa Valley is known first and foremost for its wines. But the architecture, landscape, and beautiful surroundings and views are a big part of its wine culture as well. From the beginning, proprietors of wineries and related businesses knew of the need to provide visitors with surroundings and an atmosphere that is relaxed, pleasant, and often strikingly beautiful. Providing a great ambience for experiencing wine has been a characteristic of the valley since the earliest days.

5. Hospitality: Enlightened winery owners in the valley have long recognized that one of the keys to success is to give visitors a place where they can enjoy and get to understand the vintner's wine, a place to meet other people who are similarly inclined, and a place where they can feel they are a part of the experience of the winery. Wine tasting, winery touring, and wine education have long been essential to the success of wineries and the satisfaction of winery visitors. But in addition to the wineries themselves, other businesses, notably restaurants and resorts, provide their own hospitality, which

contributes to the wine culture of the valley. Recently, dozens of restaurants have blossomed all over the valley, making it a culinary as well as a wine center. Twenty-two percent of the Michelin starred restaurants in the Bay Area were in the Napa Valley in 2009! Similarly, centers for the fine and performing arts have come to the valley, providing cultural venues for residents and guests.

Thinking about the great wine regions of the world that you may have visited all doubtless have some of the attributes listed here, but—to borrow from the parlance of the oenophile—none has quite the same blend or same level of intensity or complexity as the wine culture of the Napa Valley. These attributes of the Napa Valley wine culture have a long tradition and are the legacy of the five historical figures we will turn to now.

Charles Krug: The Legacy of Wine Excellence and Varietal Diversity

Charles Krug is such a key figure in the development of the Napa Valley wine culture that his story deserves an in-depth discussion. In many ways, he is the father of Napa Valley viticulture and oenology. Due to the turmoil taking place in Europe in the mid-1800s, many European immigrants from countries having long traditions of winemaking and wine consumption came to United States for political reasons. As Napa Valley historian Lin Weber tells us: "Charles Krug was a prototype of the bourgeois refugees of the chaotic Europe of 1848 who were entrepreneurial, educated, and skilled, and had knowledge of viticulture and winemaking because they came from some of the great winemaking areas of Europe."[33] Krug was born in Prussia in 1825. He came to America in the summer of 1847 and stayed until May 1848, when he returned to Prussia following the outbreak of revolution in Germany and began writing revolutionary articles. He became a part of an attempt to overthrow the Parliament of Germany. The attempt failed, and Krug was put in prison and then released in 1849.

He returned to the U.S. in 1851 and arrived in San Francisco on June 14, 1852. He worked there at a German-language newspaper business until 1854. For reasons lost to history, although probably related to the fact that the U.S. government was giving out tracts of land there, Krug went to Crystal Springs (the small string of lakes that can be seen today from Highway 280 south of San Francisco and which are located directly above the San Andreas Fault in San Mateo County). By settling on a government claim there, he changed the course of the history of the California wine industry. Why? Thanks to a quirk of fate, his land was located right next to a farm owned by Colonel Agoston Haraszthy, a Hungarian immigrant who, like Krug, had left Europe because of the political turmoil of the times (although he left somewhat earlier than the revolutions of 1848).

Agoston Haraszthy

The lives of Agoston Haraszthy and Charles Krug are so intertwined that you couldn't tell the story of Krug's life in the Napa Valley without giving an overview of Haraszthy's fascinating life and contribution to American viticulture. Haraszthy was born in Budapest, Hungary on August 30, 1812. He left Hungary for the U.S., becoming what is believed to be the first Hungarian to settle here. He went to Wisconsin, where he founded the oldest incorporated village in the state, Haraszthy Town. He returned to Hungary after traveling extensively throughout the U.S. After a time in Hungary, he returned to the U.S. and again settled in Wisconsin. Living in Wisconsin, Haraszthy was disappointed at not being able to establish high-quality vineyards like he remembered from his native Hungary. In 1849, his doctor advised him to move to Florida or California, and given the excitement that was going on in California in 1849, he chose the latter. In Kansas Territory, Haraszthy formed a wagon train of approximately 60 immigrants to head for California. He served as wagon master and the wagon train took a southern route, which eventually brought it to San Diego, where they arrived in December of 1849. The population of San

Diego village was then about 650 people. Haraszthy bought 160 acres and planted fruit trees.

In San Diego's first election after being chartered a city in 1850, Haraszthy was elected Sheriff of the County. Many stories portray him as a strong, if not overly stern, peace officer. In 1851, after California statehood, Haraszthy was elected to the State Assembly, then meeting in the Northern California town of Vallejo. Now that he was located in the northern part of California, Haraszthy traveled throughout the Bay Area with his eye out for a place to pursue viticulture.

In 1853, he took advantage of a federal program to claim lands in Crystal Springs and became Charles Krug's neighbor the following year. He experimented with growing wine grapes and, ever the entrepreneur, entered into a San Francisco business assaying and refining precious metals. In April 1854, the first San Francisco branch of the United States Mint opened, and Haraszthy's reputation for public service got him appointed Assayer of the Mint. In 1857, Haraszthy purchased a parcel of 16 acres in Sonoma, which had been planted with grapevines in 1834 by Salvador Vallejo (also the owner of one of the original land grants in the Napa Valley and brother of the former Mexican governor Mariano Vallejo). He named his Sonoma property Buena Vista. At last, he had found *terroir* very much suited to viticulture. He imported European vines and planted them on a hillside, rather than the valley floor, as had been the practice throughout California.

Haraszthy toured Europe in 1861 as a state viticulture commissioner and returned with between 100,000 and 200,000 vine cuttings from 1,400 grape varietals according to one account. However many varietals he actually introduced, he opened up the possibility for serious viticulture and oenology in California's most important wine regions. "By growing and crushing *Vitis vinifera* on a large commercial scale, he laid the foundation for wine industry giants like Mondavi, Krug, Heitz, Schram, and Niebaum."[34]

Haraszthy's ideas about grape varietals were also to have a major impact on the evolution of the California wine industry. While European wine regions often grew more than one varietal in the mid-1800s, just as they do today, they specialized in a small number of them. Haraszthy was willing to experiment with all varietals, a practice that has continued in California until the present day. Although flame tokay, muscat of Alexandria, seedless sultana, and black Morocco are not likely to be found growing in California vineyards today, their introduction by Haraszthy literally revolutionized the California wine industry of the day. And lovers of today's California Cabernet Sauvignon, Merlot, Chardonnay, Zinfandel, and Pinot Noir have Haraszthy's open-minded ideas about grape varietals to thank for them.

Haraszthy is also credited with introducing the rigors of science to California viticulture and oenology. Prior to Haraszthy, viticulture in California was a random trial and error affair, but he not only brought written scientific works with him to California from Europe, but actually wrote a very famous book on viticulture himself. This was also to lead to California's distinctiveness in the wine world by focusing on technical and scientific approaches to viticulture and winemaking rather than centuries of tradition and the passing down of knowledge and techniques from generation to generation, which to a great extent was the practice in Europe.

Charles Krug (continued)

Returning to the story of Charles Krug, it is obvious that he knew early on that Haraszthy had the stamp of greatness. Leaving Crystal Springs, he followed Haraszthy to San Francisco and eventually joined him in business. It was only a matter of time until the two men would leave the confines of the city and pursue their mutual destiny amongst the vines. Krug's journey to the country is best described by a historical document published about 30 years later when he was a well-respected resident of the Napa Valley.

In January 1858, Krug went to Sonoma on general business

engagements with Colonel Haraszthy and others, purchased a tract of land and set out twenty acres of vines within the next few years. In the spring of 1858, however, during his residence at Sonoma, John Patchett of Napa City, while on a visit to Sonoma made Mr. Krug a proposition to come to Napa and make up his grapes into wine. He did so, thus making the first wine ever produced in Napa County. ... He made up thus, in 1858, 1,200 gallons of wine for Mr. Patchett, crushing his grapes with a small cider press that he brought with him for the purpose.[35]

Krug apparently saw lots of opportunity in the Napa Valley, becoming a winemaker for Patchett and establishing another kind of relationship with one of the Napa Valley's prominent citizens—the daughter of the by-then-deceased Edward Bale.

In December 1860, he was married to Miss Caroline Bale, daughter of the old pioneer Dr. E.T. Bale, and immediately removed to his present place and began its improvement. He made wine there in 1861, but from grapes procured from Knight's Valley and elsewhere in the valley, as he only began to set out vines in that year, planting about twenty acres of rooted mission grapes.[36]

Those 20 acres were on the land Krug acquired as part of his wife Caroline's dowry and which today is the core property of the Charles Krug Winery.

Krug was clearly the founding father of the commercial wine industry in the Napa Valley. Part of Krug's contribution to Napa Valley viticulture was not only his being the first major vintner using traditional European techniques, but also using scientific methods in viticulture. To be sure, Krug and the Napa Valley owe a great debt of gratitude to Agoston Haraszthy, but Krug helped to develop these techniques with Haraszthy in Sonoma and was smart enough to bring them along with him when he arrived in the Napa Valley. He not only became the major producer of wine in the valley, but was its first "wine consultant." He made wine for John Patchett, George Yount, Gustave Niebaum and others. He also helped organize the small group that was struggling to establish viticulture in the valley. After the wine business had started to become an important force in the valley, Krug worked to promote the production, marketing, and scientific aspects of viticulture among vineyard owners. He and another winery owner, Henry Pellet, brought together local vintners in December of 1875 and founded the St. Helena Viticultural Club, and Krug was chairman for many years.

The St. Helena Viticultural Club came to be important in helping growers and winery owners to understand the newest and best techniques and approaches to their business, and Charles Krug consistently worked to find ways to help the advancement of viticulture in the Napa Valley. The club was a major factor in bringing leading-edge oenological techniques to the growers of the Napa Valley.

So, as Haraszthy was doing in the Sonoma Valley, Krug advanced Napa Valley viticulture by advocating techniques that would result in the production of excellent wines, and by introducing numerous grape varietals. He was the first strong advocate of the use of a diversity of great varietals. Krug's commitment to both *wine excellence* and *varietal diversity* are clearly seen in an article addressed to the "wine men" of the Napa Valley, where Krug told Napa Valley vintners, "The producer must be induced to make and sell no more inferior wine, such as made from mission and malvoisie. Nothing ruins the prices and reputation of good California wines more than the sale of inferior wines at low prices. The grape man must sell his inferior grapes and the wine man his inferior wines to the distiller."

Krug encouraged the introduction of new ideas, technology, and new varietals.

> …Much of the credit for the expansion of the wine market goes to Charles Krug. He was a man of unlimited energy, traveling to Washington, D.C., when it became necessary to oppose or gain support for a law that affected the making of wine. He rarely if

ever missed a meeting of winemakers, whether on the local, regional, or statewide level. He was Napa's ambassador to wine and conviviality.[37]

In addition to the legacy of wine quality and varietal diversity from Charles Krug, there were four other pioneering vintners who left a legacy to the Napa Valley wine culture of today: Jacob Schram, Jacob and Frederick Beringer, and Gustave Niebaum.

Jacob Schram: The Legacy of Innovation

Jacob Schram was born in Pheddersheim, Germany, near the Rhine River. He immigrated to New York at the age of 16, and he eventually became a barber. In 1852, he left New York heading west by ship and crossed the Isthmus of Panama to the Pacific. He then went to San Francisco and continued for several years working as a barber.

He first came to the Napa Valley in 1859 and continued to work as a barber full-time, but he harbored thoughts of owning vineyards. Schram was obviously limited in financial resources, but he made up for this with innovation. Most of the land under cultivation at the time was on the valley floor, where planting, cultivation, and irrigation were the easiest to accomplish. Seeing what other men of German descent had done in the Napa Valley, he purchased a large piece of land. However, it was on the steep mountainside on the north end of the valley. He called his property "Schramsberg."

Utilizing steep mountain land that others had avoided, he and his wife cleared the densely wooded hillside of the Schramsberg property and created vineyards, planting European varieties of grapevines that thrived on the hillsides. He adapted, and in some cases invented, techniques of viticulture that took advantage of the unique *terroir* of his property. He turned what was then unwanted land into successful vineyards by innovating and adapting to the new environment he and his wife encountered in the valley. Their first crush was in 1865 or 1866.

Noting the extreme temperatures during the summers in the Napa Valley, he came to the conclusion that caves would be necessary to store wines during a hot season. He discovered that the hills behind his vineyards were of soft limestone, and so he dug a system of caves to store his wines and was the first Napa Valley vintner to do so on any large scale. By the mid-1870s, Schramsberg was producing a number of varieties of wines and had managed to plant 50 acres of vines and produce 12,000 cases of wine a year. Schram actively marketed and promoted his wines, taking trips to Europe as well as the East Coast of the U.S. He had his wines entered in the major international and American competitions and won many prestigious awards.

Beringer Brothers: The Legacy of Ambience

Jacob Beringer was born in Mainz, Germany and had a good deal of experience in working with wine, beginning at a young age. He worked in wine cellars in his small hometown as well as in Berlin. After several years working in wine cellars in both Mainz and Berlin, he immigrated to the United States, arriving in 1868. He opened his own shop in New York City, probably with the help of an older brother, Frederick, who already lived in New York.

No one knows why he suddenly left New York and headed directly to the Napa Valley, but he did. No doubt he had heard about the success of Europeans in viticulture in the Napa. The fact that Charles Krug hired him to be his winemaker when Beringer arrived in 1870 in the Napa Valley suggests that is true.

Frederick came to the Napa Valley to join his brother and then purchased property north of St. Helena in 1875. The property had beautiful stone hillsides that were ideal for constructing buildings and wine storage tunnels, which they did over a period of years.

With their European backgrounds, the Beringers, like Charles Krug before them, came to appreciate the potential of the Napa Valley as a premium wine-producing area. Author William Heintz points out:

The volcanic soil was ideal for growing the varietal grapes of Europe's winemaking regions, and, best of all, the hills could be dug out to provide storage and aging tunnels that would maintain the constant temperature needed to produce fine wines. Jacob bought land with Frederick in 1875 and settled into producing wines comparable to the premium wines he had developed in Europe. In 1876, they founded Beringer Winery.[38]

Jacob Beringer's experience in winemaking with Charles Krug inspired him and his brother to select land that would enable them to produce wines in the European style and tradition. They also soon decided that they would attempt to create a beautiful place for guests to visit in an elegant, relaxing ambience.

The Beringer House, begun in 1883, was completed two years later. "Its soaring roof lines, beautiful interior woodwork, and stained-glass windows immediately made it a showplace, reminiscent of great 19th-century houses in the Rhine land."[39] In short, the Beringers not only continued the tradition of European excellence in winemaking begun by Krug and then Schram, they also carried over the European tradition of providing visitors with an ambience of elegance, which remains their legacy to the valley to this very day.

The Beringer Vineyards' website *History & Commitments to Quality* notes:

> The Beringer brothers built their winery against a hill ... while preparing the road up to the new winemaking facility, Jacob found that the hillside behind it was solid limestone. His neighbor up the road, Jacob Schram, had demonstrated that limestone caves were ideal for storing wine because they maintained an even temperature throughout the year ... Frederick Beringer joined his brother in 1883 and began building the Rhine House—a temple of sorts to the cult of elegance that began to surround the juice of the grape. Two years later they planted a row of elm trees along both sides of the country road. The attitude of old world refinement that these men portrayed (and in fact possessed) set a style that has continued to the present day in many of the region's wineries.[40]

The Rhine House remains one of the most beautiful buildings in the Napa Valley and has inspired many vintners to make beautiful architecture and a pleasing ambience a part of their winery estates.

Gustave Niebaum: The Legacy of Hospitality

Gustave Niebaum was born in Helsinki, Finland. He went to sea when he was in his 20s and became the captain of a ship at an early age. He went to the Arctic and Alaska in the late 1850s, where he was very successful hunting and trading furs. He arrived in San Francisco with more than half a million dollars worth of furs. He immediately attracted the attention of the elite in the city and became involved in several businesses.

Like the other European-born pioneers of the Napa Valley wine business, Niebaum had wine knowledge and a European perspective of viticulture and winemaking. Though his native Finland did not have the climate for growing grapes, he became intrigued with prospects of the Napa Valley as a wine-producing region. He purchased a vineyard estate named Inglenook, and began operations sometime around 1880. (A newspaper account credits Charles Krug and E. B. Smith with first making wine in Niebaum's winery in 1879.)

Niebaum was an extremely intelligent and capable man with an inquisitive mind and unbounded self-confidence. He spoke five languages: Russian, German, French, English, and Finnish. Napa Valley historian Lin Weber points out that Niebaum:

> …taught himself all the world had to say about viticulture and oenology. He imported samples of soil from various locations in Europe for comparison with the several types of soil on his estate. He planted cuttings from numerous varietals and made careful records of all he observed. He inspected European winemaking facilities and visited technical schools on the continent. He believed that everything about a winery should be first rate, reflecting an attitude of elegance and European ease.

His 'sample room' where visitors could taste the wine he made was lavishly appointed with ornate curve of woodworking, fine crystal and stained-glass windows...[41]

Niebaum's early version of a tasting room was not the first in the Napa Valley, but it was the first to explicitly emphasize *hospitality.* It was carefully and extravagantly designed to show off Niebaum's wines and estate in the very best way possible, and doubtlessly set the standard for winery tasting rooms in the future.

Lin Weber captured the impact and significance of Inglenook's sampling room when she observed:

There really was nothing like this room anywhere in the wine industry in California. Niebaum intended to entertain in the grand style, to impress his visitors and perhaps the press. With Inglenook, valley winemaking advanced a giant step towards producing and marketing the highest quality wine.[42]

Niebaum also made two other contributions to the evolution of winemaking in the Napa Valley. First, he was fastidious about cleanliness and sanitary conditions in the winery, significantly enhancing the quality and reliability of his wines. Second, his was the first winery in the Napa Valley to bottle all of its wines (Napa Valley wines were sold in casks in those days), something that had previously not been done by any wineries in the valley because it was very expensive to do at the time.

From 1860, when Charles Krug first planted grapes on his estate, until 1879, when he was attributed with making the first wine for Gustave Niebaum's Inglenook vineyard, the Napa Valley looked as if it were well on its way to having both a thriving wine industry and wine culture in the American era. But the valley was to face a series of devastating crises that would hold it back for almost a century until it finally began to take its place as one of the great wine regions of the world.

Chapter V Appendix:

People, Places, and Things During the Development of the Wine Industry and Wine Culture of the Napa Valley in the American Period

There was a perfect storm for the development of a wine industry that began in the Napa Valley in 1848. The causes: new government land use policies breaking up the large landholdings from the Mexican era that came with the American annexation of California; the Gold Rush, which eventually resulted in the influx of hundreds of thousands of diverse and often skilled people to California; land squatting not only in the gold country but in adjacent areas; and the unsuccessful European revolutions of 1848, which resulted in many men arriving in California from the wine-loving areas of Europe with winemaking interests and skills. Before it occurred in the Napa Valley, this perfect storm happened in the adjacent Sonoma Valley, even before it did in the Napa Valley, due to the arrival there of Agoston Haraszthy and Charles Krug.

Agoston Haraszthy

- *Agoston Haraszthy was born in Budapest, Hungary in 1812. He left Hungary for the U.S. and was the first Hungarian to settle in the U.S. He founded the oldest incorporated village in Wisconsin, called Haraszthy*

Town. He returned to Hungary because of the 1848 political disruptions. He returned to Wisconsin, but in 1849, at his doctor's advice (he had asthma), moved to the warmer climate in California.

- *He formed a wagon train in Kansas Territory and took it to San Diego. Haraszthy bought 160 acres and planted fruit trees. In 1850, he was elected the first sheriff of San Diego County. He was eventually elected to the State Assembly, which met in Vallejo in Northern California. In 1853, he got a federal grant and moved to Crystal Springs, where he eventually met Charles Krug, who became his neighbor the following year.*

- *In 1857, Haraszthy purchased 16 acres in Sonoma, which had been planted with grapevines by Salvador Vallejo in 1834, and named the property "Buena Vista." He imported European vines and toured Europe in 1861 as a state viticulture commissioner, returning with thousands of vine cuttings from many varietals. He experimented with all varietals he could find and introduced the rigors of science to California viticulture and oenology. Haraszthy made bad financial decisions and was forced to file for bankruptcy. He went to Nicaragua to start another business and, in 1869, disappeared in a river on his Nicaraguan property. His body was never found.*

Charles Krug

- ***Charles Krug*** *is the father of Napa Valley viticulture and oenology. A political refugee from Prussia who took part in an* *attempt to overthrow the Germany Parliament, he was imprisoned and released in 1849. He came to the U.S. in 1851, and to San Francisco in 1852. He received a land grant at Crystal Springs next to a farm owned by Agoston Haraszthy. He followed Haraszthy to San Francisco and eventually joined him in business. He moved to the Sonoma Valley with Haraszthy to pursue viticulture, acquiring 20 acres of vines. In 1858, John Patchett of Napa convinced Krug to come to Napa Valley to make wine for him. In 1860, Krug married Caroline Bale, daughter of Edward Bale, and acquired 20 acres of Bale's land as part of his wife's dowry. Following Haraszthy's example, he used traditional European techniques and scientific methods in viticulture. He became the major producer of wine in Napa Valley and helped organize groups that were struggling to establish viticulture there, co-founding the St. Helena Viticultural Club in 1875. He advocated techniques for production of excellent wines and introduced numerous grape varietals.*

Jacob Schram

- *Jacob Schram was born in Pheddersheim, Germany in 1826 and immigrated to New York at the age of 16. He became a barber and, in 1852, left New York by ship heading west crossing the*

Isthmus of Panama to the Pacific, arriving in San Francisco in 1852 and going to work in the young city as a barber.

• *Schram came to Napa Valley in 1859 and continued to work as a barber full-time, but he harbored thoughts of owning vineyards. He purchased a large, steep piece of mountainside land on the north end of the Valley and called it "Schramsberg." He planted varieties of wine grapes favored in Europe at the time that thrived on the hillsides. Adapting techniques of viticulture that took advantage of the unique terroir of his property, Schram dug a system of caves to store and protect his wines during the hot season.*

Jacob and Fredrick Beringer

• *Jacob Beringer was born in Mainz, Germany, in 1845. By age 15, he had accumulated a good deal of wine experience from working in wine cellars in his small hometown as well as in Berlin. He immigrated to the United States, arriving in 1868. He left New York and came to the Napa Valley in 1870, and Charles Krug hired him to be his winemaker in the Napa Valley. Frederick Beringer came to the Napa Valley from New York in 1875 to join his brother and purchased property north of St. Helena. Jacob bought land with Frederick in 1875, and they began producing wines comparable to*

105

the European wines they knew from Germany. They founded Beringer Winery in 1876. The brothers decided to create a beautiful place for guests to visit and the Rhine House was completed in 1885.

Gustave Niebaum

• ***Gustave Niebaum*** *was born in Helsinki, Finland, in 1842. He went to sea when he was in his 20s and became the captain of a ship at an early age. He was a very successful hunter and fur trader in the Arctic and Alaska in the late 1850s.*

• *Niebaum arrived in San Francisco with more than half a million dollars worth of furs. He had knowledge of the European perspective on viticulture and winemaking and purchased a vineyard estate named "Inglenook." Charles Krug made wine in Niebaum's winery in 1879. He imported samples of soil from Europe for comparison with the soil on his estate and planted cuttings from numerous varietals, taking careful records of all he observed.*

• *Niebaum's tasting room was not the first in the Napa Valley, but his was the first in which hospitality was emphasized. His tasting room was designed to show off his wines and estate. He emphasized cleanliness and sanitary conditions in the winery, enhancing the quality and reliability of his wines, and Inglenook was the first winery in the Napa Valley to bottle all of its wines.*

Chapter VI

Struggles and Triumphs in the Later Period of the American Era

In the 40-plus years from George Yount's first land grant in the Napa Valley in 1836 to Gustave Niebaum first opening a "sample room" at his Inglenook Winery in the 1880s, the valley went from wilderness to wine country. The Napa Valley was far from the largest wine-producing region in the state, but hundreds of wineries were in operation; an infrastructure of wine associations and cooperatives were in place; and the traditions of wine excellence, varietal diversity, winery ambience, and hospitality that are the hallmarks of the wine culture of the Napa Valley up until this day had been established by the pioneers of the valley's wine industry.

One would have thought that the valley was well on its way to taking its place among the world's great wine-producing regions, but this was not to be. A long series of negative historical events—both natural and manmade—would set back the development of a true world-class wine business almost a full century!

Pestilence, Prohibition, and Wars

The first of these historical catastrophes was devastating not only for the Napa Valley but for viticulture in the rest of the U.S. and Europe as well. It turns out that living in the soil in some places east

108

of the Rockies in North America is a louse called phylloxera that destroys the root system of grapevines. Over the centuries, many grapevine species native to North America had evolved to become resistant to phylloxera, but the Old World *Vitis vinifera* vines that produced wine grapes in California, Europe, and other parts of the world, were defenseless.

Thanks to new avenues of trade to California, or perhaps phylloxera's own natural migration, it had begun to infest the mission vines brought in by the Spanish priests. Also infested were the other European varietals brought into California and planted there by Agoston Haraszthy in Sonoma, Charles Krug in the Napa Valley, and other enlightened early California viticulturists. Of even greater consequence to the entire world wine business, native American species of grapevines were sent to Europe to be experimented with, and they brought with them their deadly cargo of phylloxera lice. It is hard to unravel the routes taken by the deadly lice, but the phylloxera epidemic was actually discovered in French vineyards in the late 1860s, which predates its discovery in Napa in 1872.

Regardless of where or when it first occurred, phylloxera infestation now virtually threatened to destroy *Vitis vinifera* viticulture throughout the world. In the final two decades of the 19th century, phylloxera threatened the blossoming wine industry in the Napa Valley. Every type of remedy was tried, including the flooding of the vineyards and the use of poisonous gases, but nothing worked.

Eventually, it was discovered that a *Vitis vinifera* grapevine that was grafted to the rootstalk of a North American species retained its own desirable fruit characteristics while the stock and root system of the American varietal below the graft protected it from the phylloxera lice in the soil. The havoc that resulted from the infestation—the time-consuming experimentation with solutions to the problem, the necessity of ripping up vineyards infested with phylloxera and often replacing them with other crops—set the Napa Valley wine industry back decades. Phylloxera continued to wreak havoc in the Napa

Valley wine industry many years into the 20th century. Less than half of the grapevines planted in the 1800s in the valley survived into the 1900s. In addition, Napa Valley grapes and wines had not attained the level of prestige that would have demanded high prices in the market. Vintners were forced to either abandon winemaking altogether and rip out their vineyards in favor of other crops, or continued to struggle through the early 1900s.

The outbreak of World War I was a challenge for the economy of the entire nation and did not help the wine industry in the Napa Valley. Then came perhaps the greatest challenge of all in the form of the 18th Amendment to the United States Constitution. It was ratified on January 16, 1919, and it ushered in Prohibition on January 16, 1920. It doesn't take much imagination to see how devastating the prohibition of the sale of alcohol was on the viticulture industry in the already-struggling Napa Valley. Although many wineries had no choice but to close or convert to other enterprises, some managed to get contracts with the Catholic Church to make sacramental wine. This was legal under the Volstead Act, which was implemented to enforce Prohibition. Another loophole for Napa Valley viticulturists was section 29 of the Volstead Act, which authorized the home production for personal consumption of small amounts of fermented fruit juices, so some vintners in the valley sold grapes or grape juice primarily to families who had migrated to the United States from the wine-drinking areas of Europe. Regrettably though, this often required using grape varietals that had thicker skins and thus could tolerate bulk shipping, or varietals that could withstand dilution with water. Some wineries that managed to survive the Prohibition era using one or more of the techniques described above included: Charles Krug, Beringer Brothers, Christian Brothers (operating from Benicia during Prohibition), Beaulieu Vineyard (which was founded by Frenchman Georges de Latour only a decade before Prohibition was enacted) and a few others. But Prohibition did lead to the demise of Jacob Schram's Schramsberg and Gustave Niebaum's Inglenook.

America's biggest failed social experiment proved to almost destroy what had resulted in the founding of hundreds of vineyards and wineries in the middle and late 19th century. Coming as it did on the heels of the phylloxera plague, Prohibition was devastating to the wine industry of the Napa Valley. But happily, even Prohibition was not enough to extinguish viticulture from the valley completely. Only about 60 Napa Valley properties that could be said to be truly operating as vineyards and wineries survived Prohibition. Of those wineries, the vast majority were producing bulk wines often sold to out-of-state bottlers, or wine in barrels sold to retailers. And the vast majority of wine that was produced in the Napa Valley came from vineyards full of inferior grape varietals.

After the repeal of Prohibition in 1933, a small handful of men, and at least one woman, went to work to put the valley back on the trajectory it had been on prior to the onset of phylloxera in the 1880s. While the quality wine industry in the valley remained extremely small during the period immediately after the repeal of Prohibition, that period did produce individuals who today take their rightful place in the pantheon of Napa Valley wine producers. Niebaum died in 1908, and his winery was shut down after Prohibition went into effect. However, Niebaum's widow, Suzanne, wealthy from her inheritance of his estate, reopened Inglenook shortly after the repeal of Prohibition. In these times, the wine industry throughout California was all but emaciated. However, Suzanne Niebaum found a wine marketing and operations wonder named Carl Bundschu, and then brought on board her great-nephew, John Daniel Jr. They went to work to upgrade the vineyards and the winemaking operations. Unlike virtually every winery in the valley at the time that sold only bulk wines in barrels, Inglenook bottled their best-quality wines. Many of these were single varietal, and all of their bottled wines carried the Napa Valley label. John Daniel Jr. took over operations in 1939, and Inglenook was reestablished as a fine wine producer.

Another of the heroes of the era immediately following the repeal of Prohibition was Georges de Latour. His Beaulieu Vineyard had not existed in the 1800s. A native of France who had migrated to United

States at age 26, he started from very humble beginnings producing wine in the Napa Valley not long before the beginning of Prohibition. When it arrived, he survived it by getting contracts to sell sacramental wine to the Catholic Church. He was not only an astute businessman but also someone with grape growing and winemaking instincts and talents, and a desire for producing fine wine.

In the early days after the repeal of Prohibition, Beaulieu Vineyard's business consisted mostly of bulk wine. But de Latour had also made fine premium bottled wine even before the repeal and continued to do so until the end of his career. On a trip to France in 1937, he hired winemaker Andre Tchelistcheff, another wine luminary from the period immediately after Prohibition. Tchelistcheff helped de Latour to modernize his operation and continuously grow a fine wine production at Beaulieu, and he was a major force in the Napa Valley wine industry until his retirement in 1973. Among his many credits were: pioneering the process of aging wine in small French oak barrels, defining a style for high-quality California Cabernet Sauvignon, and initiating the program for "Private Reserve" Cabernet wine at Beaulieu.

Any discussion of the period needs also to include Brother Timothy and the Christian Brothers Winery. He was teaching science in Catholic schools in the Bay Area and Sacramento during Prohibition but transferred to Mont La Salle in Napa in 1935 to become the wine chemist for the local Christian Brothers order that had been making sacramental wine. Under the guidance of Brother Timothy, the Christian Brothers Winery began producing quality wines beginning in the late 1930s, which served to enhance the reputation of the Napa Valley. The order bought Greystone Cellars, the current home of the Culinary Institute of America. Brother Timothy lived to be 94 years old and was an ambassador of Napa Wine for 70 years. He is recognized as one of the most influential men in the California wine industry during the 20th Century.

All told, the number of people involved in making fine or even good wine in the Napa Valley in the period after Prohibition was quite small. Wine historian James Lapsley tells us that Andre Tchelistcheff said there were only four "outstanding wine processing plants" in the valley after Prohibition was repealed: Inglenook, Beaulieu, Larkmead, and Beringer. Lapsley himself adds to that group the Christian Brothers Winery and Louis Martini Winery, whose owner and namesake built a state-of-the-art winery in 1933, the first winery built in the valley following Prohibition, after having produced sacramental wines during Prohibition elsewhere in the state.

Even though those wineries and the people behind them are still recognized as legendary today, they represent all that was left of the Napa Valley quality wine industry after the devastation wrought by Prohibition. And Prohibition overlapped the Great Depression, which was followed by World War II, and finally the Korean War. It wasn't until the Eisenhower era that sustained economic activity began to fuel economic growth in the U.S., and that applied to the Napa Valley as well. And amazingly, the properties of the men who created the Napa Valley wine culture in the first place in the 19th century would all eventually play a key role in the ultimate ascension of Napa Valley wines and wine culture on the world stage.

The Role of the Legacy Wine Properties in the Rise of Napa Valley Wines and Wine Culture

The historic Charles Krug Winery, founded in 1860, left the legacy of *quality wines* and *varietal diversity* to the Napa Valley in the latter half of the 19th century. Despite all of the hardships of the period from the 1880s until the 1950s, the property managed to remain intact after Krug's death in 1892, although not under the ownership of the Krug family. It continued to produced vines and grapes, thanks especially to contracts with the Catholic Church during Prohibition. However, because of all the troubled times, the

Charles Krug Winery never reached the potential that one would have imagined after seeing it under the supervision of Charles Krug himself.

Things began to change in 1943, when an Italian family from Lodi called the Mondavis purchased the Charles Krug property and began to slowly build it back to the stature it deserved. Incidentally, this was not an isolated case. Since the repeal of Prohibition, Italian winemakers (such as the Gallo Brothers in Modesto, the Sebastianis in Sonoma, Louis Martini, and the Trincheros in Napa) were spreading out all over California, carrying out the winemaking traditions of their mother country. When Cesare Mondavi, the patriarch of the Mondavi family, died in 1959, his wife, Rosa, was named president of the company. She is now a part of Napa Valley legend. Her son, Peter, took over the Charles Krug Winery and his son, Robert, founded his own Robert Mondavi Winery down Highway 29 in Oakville.

Beginning in the second half of the 20th century, the Charles Krug Winery pioneered over the decades such quality wine production techniques as: vintage dating of varietal wines, cold fermentation for white wines, cold sterile, filtration, and fermentation in small glass-lined tanks. Today, the valley is full of wineries that have made their reputations following the valley's tradition of emphasizing quality in both viticulture and oenology, a tradition begun by Charles Krug well over a century ago.

Certainly the most historic testimonial to the tradition of quality wine from the Napa Valley came at the famous Judgment of Paris. It took place on May 24, 1976, and Napa Valley wines from Stag's Leap Wine Cellars and Chateau Montelena defeated the best French wines in a tasting for the first time in history. From that day forward, Napa Valley vintners have not only strived for the highest wine quality, but more and more have been recognized for it. Credit for this reputation for wine quality goes to a number of people over many years, but it had its roots in the work done by Charles Krug beginning almost exactly a century and a half ago.

Of course, Robert Mondavi could lay claim to pioneering many techniques that led to dramatic increases in wine quality as well, but perhaps one of his greatest innovations had to do with varietal diversity. Even though he had long since left the Charles Krug Winery by that time, Robert Mondavi made what was arguably one of the two greatest contributions to American varietal differentiation with his "Fumé Blanc" version of the Sauvignon Blanc.

In 1968, Mondavi produced a dry, oaked Sauvignon Blanc, and came up with the name "Fumé Blanc." Mondavi offered to allow anyone to use the name Fumé Blanc for that style of Sauvignon Blanc, and a varietal that was hardly known as a single varietal wine became a huge success. Robert Mondovi was the man most responsible for promoting the labeling of Napa Valley wines varietally rather than generically, and this eventually became the standard for New World wines.

The other major contribution to varietal diversity of the magnitude of Fumé Blanc would be White Zinfandel, first developed be the Trinchero family at Sutter Home. In the 1970s, Sutter Home began producing a white wine from Zinfandel grapes by bleeding off and fermenting separately some juice in order to increase the intensity of their red Zinfandel wine. By 1975, they were producing an off-dry white wine from Zinfandel grapes that was extremely popular with the public. While neither Fumé Blanc nor White Zinfandel have garnered critical praise among wine writers and critics, it must be said that if they have done nothing else, they have served to educate the wine market as to the importance of varietal diversity in the Napa Valley wine culture.

Many others began pioneering the marketing of diverse varietals, such as Peter Newton, founder of Sterling Vineyards, who produced the first vintage dated Merlot in California in 1969, while also cultivating Chardonnay and Sauvignon Blanc in these early years. Today, many Napa Valley wineries have a number of varietals in their portfolios that they can offer visitors to the winery, retail buyers, and wine club members. This is due to the Mondavis' and other vintners' efforts to promote varietal diversity in the decades after the repeal of Prohibition.

Another of the wineries from the 18th century that was responsible for a part of the legacy of the Napa Valley wine culture—winemaking innovation—was Jacob Schram's Schramsberg Winery. History did not treat the Schramsberg estate as well as it did the Krug estate. After Jacob Schram's death in 1905, Jacob's son, Herman, tried to carry on the family business but was essentially defeated by phylloxera and Prohibition. The property changed hands a number of times and did not function as a true vineyard estate again until it was purchased by Jack and Jamie Davies in 1965.

The Davies intended to reestablish Schramsberg as a quality winery. Somehow, they drew from the spirit of innovation which was the legacy that Jacob Schram had left to the Napa Valley when he was the first to utilize hillside property and build caves to help preserve his wine. Instead of relying on the varietals that were popular at the time that they purchased the Schramsberg property, the Davies decided to produce America's premiere sparkling wine, made in the French style of champagne but with subtle California differences.

Amazingly, the Schramsberg property, which had led the way to innovation in Napa Valley viticulture in the late 1800s, was now being used in the same way by its new owners almost a century later. Many other Napa Valley vintners have shown similar innovation in the years since Prohibition's repeal. Wine historian James Lapsley cites these innovations that originated or were readily adapted in the Napa Valley, beginning in the late 1940s: cold fermentation, inert storage containers of glass or stainless steel, blanketing of wines with carbon dioxide or nitrogen, the use of bentonite for protein stability, modern bottling techniques, techniques for controlling and managing malolactic fermentation, the introduction of new French oak, and the introduction of pure yeast cultures.

Of the four properties that set the standard for today's Napa Valley wine culture, the one that managed to survive all of the difficult times in the valley was the Beringer brothers' vineyards. Today, the Beringer Vineyards is the oldest continuous operating winery in the Napa Valley. Thankfully, it still maintains a beautiful ambience created by its founders, Jacob and Frederick Beringer. While it has gone through a number of owners (and is currently owned by the Foster's Brewing Company of Australia), all of the owners through the years have obviously recognized the magnificent ambience of the property and have meticulously maintained it for the enjoyment of its visitors. Once again, one of the Napa Valley's legacy vineyards is today maintaining its original heritage. With the stately buildings and beautiful trees, one can hardly imagine that it will ever cease to be a place where visitors to the Napa Valley seek the beautiful ambience that the valley offers.

Many beautiful properties have joined the Beringer Vineyards in the Napa Valley over the years, so it can no longer exclusively hold claim to being the most beautiful. Today, the list of Napa Valley wineries that have followed the example of the Beringers in providing a beautiful ambience to their visitors is long indeed. From the artistic experience at the Hess Collection or Clos Pegase, to the architecture of Spring Mountain Vineyard or Opus One, to the vistas enjoyed at Artesa or Sterling, or any of the dozens of wineries lining the hills of the Napa Valley.

Producer/director Francis Ford Coppola purchased the old Inglenook property in 1975 after it had struggled as a winery with several owners who relied primarily on the Inglenook brand (originally established by Gustave Niebaum) to see it through tough times. Coppola renamed the winery Niebaum-Coppola in honor of its founder because he felt an affinity for the man who made a fortune in a completely different endeavor before turning his passion to wine.

Hospitality was a primary consideration at Niebaum's Inglenook Winery, and Coppola must have felt an affinity to hospitality as well. When he changed the name of his winery in 2006 to the Rubicon Winery in honor of his wine brand, he focused on hospitality just as Niebaum did. The Rubicon VIP visitor experience now includes a visit to the restored estate, a legacy historical tour, access to the historic Chateau and wine library, and a visit to the Centennial Museum with articles from both wine and cinema history on display.

This program is another step in the evolution of hospitality at valley wineries, but there are many other excellent hospitality experiences at such wineries as Domain Chandon, Robert Mondavi, Sterling, and many others that are a continuation of the tradition started at Inglenook in the 19th century. And hospitality at Napa Valley wineries is a large part of what makes the Napa Valley the second largest destination (next to Disneyland) in California.

This examination of the history of wine and the wine culture of the Napa Valley tells us that from long before recorded history the valley possessed the natural elements of *terroir*, the soil and weather conditions, to make it potentially a special place in the world of wine. But it took a unique social, political and individual human history, along with individual struggles and triumphs, to get to today's Napa Valley wine industry and wine culture. The Napa Valley has an abundance of quality wines, different wine varietals, beautiful ambience, and phenomenal hospitality at its hundreds of wineries, but this did not occur spontaneously or instantly. Knowing the story of how this all came about should help the visitor to enjoy all aspects of the Napa Valley wine culture, not just the wine itself.

Chapter VI Appendix:

People, Places, and Things During the Later Period of the American Era

After the Gold Rush, the wine industry became firmly established in the Napa Valley. However, a series of disastrous events occurred that stifled the development of the premium wine industry in the valley for almost three-quarters of a century.

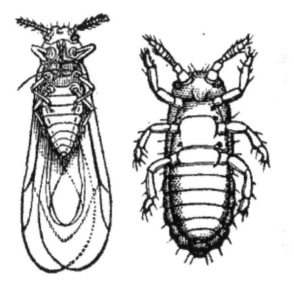

Phylloxera Plant Lice

- *Phylloxera, an almost microscopic plant louse native to the Mississippi Valley, proved devastatingly destructive to European Vitis vinifera grapevines. Its actual path of migration is unknown, but it probably traveled to France on native North American vines brought there for experimentation in the late 1850s and arrived in Northern California via imported French vines in the 1860s. Many methods were attempted to control phylloxera, and by the late 1870s, it was determined that grafting vinifera vines onto resistant native American rootstock was the only viable answer. The* *phylloxera infestations of the late 1800s almost completely destroyed the wine industry in France and other European countries, and while not as destructive in Northern California, half of the vines planted since their introduction into the valley by George Yount did not survive into the 20th century thanks to phylloxera.*

* *Unfortunately, the phylloxera louse returned to the Napa Valley after the wine industry had been reestablished and was flourishing in the 1970s and 1980s. During that time, there was a dramatic increase in the planting of vines in the valley because of the resurgence of demand for Napa Valley wine. Many of those vines were grafted to AXR 1 rootstock, which had been field-tested by the University of California since the 1890s and was thought to be resistant to phylloxera. Unfortunately, that proved not to be true. In the 1980s and 1990s, more than two-thirds of the valley's acreage had to be replanted at an estimated cost of approximately three billion dollars.*

* *Fortunately, the inventive generation of vintners that had arisen in the Napa Valley at the time was able not only to withstand the financial burden, but also used the opportunity to use new techniques, get smarter about cultivation based on research done at universities in the decades since Prohibition, and introduce new varietals and clones to the valley that amazingly made the valley better off for having suffered this second phylloxera infestation. Cultivation decisions and actions that were made necessary by the replanting of phylloxera-infested vines in the 1980s and 1990s resulted in the dominance of Cabernet Sauvignon acreage in the middle and upper valley, and the removal of chardonnay from those areas to the cooler Carneros area, where Pinot Noir also became well established.*

Harvesting Blackberries Instead of Grapes In Post-Prohibition Napa Valley *(Photo courtesy of Napa County Historical Society)*

- *Since the initial outbreak of phylloxera, the Napa Valley wine industry was to endure two world wars and several smaller wars and economic downturns, but the biggest jolt to the industry was the 18th Amendment to the U.S. Constitution. It prohibited the sale, manufacture, and transportation of alcohol for consumption. It lasted from 1919 until 1933, with the ratification of the 21st Amendment, which repealed the 18th Amendment. During this period, the wine industry virtually ceased to exist in the Napa Valley, with only a handful of wineries continuing to make wine for either sacramental purposes or illegal purposes. As a result of both the phylloxera infestation and Prohibition, thousands of acres of vineyards in the Napa Valley were ripped out and replaced by fruit orchards, wheat and hay production, livestock production, and even silk production.*

- *During Prohibition and even after its repeal in 1933, no new wineries opened in the Napa Valley. Economic conditions brought on by both the Depression, World War II, followed by the Korean War, suffocated the wine industry in the Napa Valley.*

Louis Martini

- *A number of vintners of Italian descent came to California and used the skills and techniques which originated in their mother country. **Louis Martini** began to make wine as a very young man, and when he was 19, his father sent him back to Italy to study winemaking. In 1933, his built the first new winery in the Napa Valley since the beginning of Prohibition and was a 20th century pioneer in producing quality wines in the valley.*

Robert and Peter Mondavi

- *Each of the wineries founded in the 19th century by men who led the way in defining the wine culture of the Napa Valley were* *dramatically affected by the pestilence, Prohibition, and wars that impacted the valley from the end of the 19ᵗʰ through the middle of the 20ᵗʰ century. For example, the Charles Krug Winery remained intact after his death though it was no longer owned by his family. The property continued as an operating winery through Prohibition by producing sacramental wines and was a much lesser winery after Krug's departure.*

- *In 1943, Cesare Mondavi, the head of an Italian immigrant family living in the Central Valley and working as an independent fruit shipper, bought the Charles Krug Winery and began making quality bottled wines. His two sons, **Robert and Peter Mondavi**, were given 12% of the winery business and were both influential in the development and success of the winery. Although they were to have a severe rift, resulting in Robert leaving to start his own winery, both of the Mondavi brothers contributed tremendously to the revival of the legacy of wine excellence and varietal diversity established by Charles Krug in the previous century.*

Jack and Jamie Davies   **Hugh Davies**

- *The Schramsberg estate changed hands after Jacob Schram's death, but was unable to succeed as a functioning winery through Prohibition. It was in a state of decay when it was purchased by **Jack and Jamie Davies** in 1965.*

- *The Davies, like Jacob Schram, showed a high degree of innovation by choosing to produce sparkling wine on their property. Their son **Hugh Davies** is today continuing in the tradition of his parents, and Jacob Schram before them.*

The Rhine House at Beringer Vineyards

- *The winery of Jacob and Fredrick Beringer survived the Prohibition era (by making sacramental wine for the Catholic Church) and continued to operate successfully throughout the 20th century and into the 21st. It is now the longest continuously operating winery in the Napa Valley. The winery did not stay in the hands of the Beringer family for long, however, and has had several owners during its history.*

- *Fortunately, all of its owners have appreciated the beautiful ambience that the Beringer brothers created, and have respected and taken care of its beautiful grounds and buildings. Its current owner, the Foster's Group, has recently restored and refurbished the Rhine House, an iconic historical Napa Valley building.*

John Daniel Jr.

- *The Inglenook Winery, founded by Gustave Niebaum, was closed by Prohibition, but his* widow, *Suzanne, reopened it shortly after its repeal. She was joined at Inglenook by her great-nephew,* **John Daniel Jr.,** *in 1939. Under his leadership, Inglenook was reestablished as a fine wine producer, and he is recognized as one of the prime movers in the revitalization of the Napa Valley wine industry.*

Francis Ford Coppola

- *After the era of John Daniel Jr., the quality of Inglenook wine began to decline and the property was divided. The Academy*

125

Award-winning film director **Francis Ford Coppola** *purchased the Inglenook property in 1975 and renamed it and the brand Niebaum-Coppola in honor of its founder. Coppola has since changed the name of the property to Rubicon and continued Gustave Niebaum's legacy of hospitality by introducing a visitor experience at the winery that befits a Hollywood film legend.*

Afterword

History and Wine Tasting in Today's Napa Valley

History is fun in and of itself, but hopefully we are also able to learn something from our past that we can apply in our everyday lives today. Sometimes what we learn from history can even make our lives a little more fun. This book has tried to provide the reader with a concise source of knowledge and an appreciation for a small and beautiful valley that has played such an important role in the history of the state of California, and has certainly made its mark on the wine world. Knowledge of the valley's rich historical legacy and vibrant wine culture and a little preparation can contribute a lot to the enjoyment of a visit to the Napa Valley.

The Napa Valley is, of course, more than just the place where some of the world's greatest wines are produced. It is also a destination for millions of people from all over the world who come to taste, learn about, and purchase the Napa Valley's sought-after wines. They also come to enjoy the beauty of the valley and wineries, as well as the magnificent cuisine that can now be found in the many distinguished restaurants. And they come to enjoy the amenities of the hotels and spas that have come to be a part of the Napa Valley experience. An oft-quoted statistic about the Napa Valley is that it is the second largest tourist destination in the state of California behind Disneyland, with over five million visitors exploring up and down Highway 29 and the Silverado Trail through the Napa Valley each year. While both are leading tourist attractions, the Napa Valley and Disneyland differ in many ways, and perhaps the most important is that there are no turnstiles at the entrance to the Napa Valley. Once inside the gates of Disneyland, you are provided with all sorts of printed information, maps, and visual cues that guide you through the experiences that the park has to offer. This is not so in the Napa Valley. When you arrive here, you are on your own.

Many people arrive in the valley without any plan. They have the expectation that their visit will be structured as it would be at Disneyland or other theme parks or attractions owned and operated by one large entity. There are many tourist maps available from sources like the Napa Valley Conference and Visitors Bureau at their Napa Valley Visitor Information Center in downtown Napa (1310 Napa Town Center). There are also lists of wineries at their website www.napavalley.com. But with approximately 500 wineries listed on that website, help is needed to sort things out and make the trip to the valley as enjoyable and rewarding as possible. There are tools on the Internet that can help you explore the Napa Valley wine culture, which is the legacy of over 150 years of viticulture and winemaking, with roots that go back to the Spanish period in California. The five attributes of the Napa Valley wine culture discussed in the previous chapters really constitute the DNA of the Napa Valley, and everyone who comes to visit should weigh the importance of each of the attributes for themselves and then plan their trip accordingly.

For example, there are people who come to the valley *on a mission!* They are Cabernet lovers from, let's say, the Midwest, where they cannot find Napa Valley Cabs at retail outlets, and they come to taste specific wines and vintages to buy in quantity to ship home to fill their wine cellars. For those visitors, the job is relatively easy and limited to finding the wineries that make the type of wine they will love. But suppose this visitor is accompanied by a spouse, family, or friends who are less passionate about Napa Valley Cabs and more interested in tasting and learning about new kinds of wines, enjoying scenic vistas, or experiencing beautiful surroundings and art. Then our hypothetical valley visitor would be well advised to allot some time to going to some wineries that exhibit some of the other attributes of the Napa Valley wine culture in addition to wine excellence.

Even though there are about 500 wineries in the Napa Valley, the most that the average visitor should plan to visit in a single day is three or four. Wineries generally open at 10:00 a.m., and most of us are not much interested in tasting wine before midmorning anyway. It is hard to imagine discovering, exploring, and enjoying all that a good Napa Valley winery has to offer in less than an hour and a half. So, in doing the math (and including some time to enjoy a lunch at one of the valley's wonderful restaurants), four wineries is certainly the upper limit of wineries that can be visited in a single day.

With that in mind, before coming to the valley, a visitor who has read this book can determine how many wineries they could reasonably plan on visiting during a stay in the valley. The visitor could then decide, in percentage terms, how important each attribute of the valley's wine culture is to them and the others who will be making the trip. Having gone through this simple exercise before the trip, the visitor can begin to decide which wineries to visit. Fortunately, the Internet provides a number of tools to help decide that and tips on how to map out an itinerary. Of course there is always the possibility of serendipity happening (people at one winery will often suggest another once they have found out about your preferences), and things needn't be completely structured, but it is much better to come to the valley with a general plan in mind rather than expecting someone to tell you where to go when you arrive.

General Tools

The Napa Valley Vintners Association website (www.napavintners.com) has excellent interactive maps of the valley (one with all wineries, one with wineries open to the public, and one with wineries open by appointment), which, when used in conjunction with a mapping site like google.com/maps or mapquest.com, will provide directions to wineries and distances between wineries. The site only includes wineries that are members of the Vintners Association, but there are over 300 of them, and most quality wineries in the valley are members.

1. Wine Excellence

This attribute of the Napa Valley wine culture was first pioneered by Charles Krug when the little wine that was being made in the Napa Valley was of uneven quality and usually made from mission grapes. Today, the quality of Napa Valley wines is by far the most important aspect of the valley's wine culture and what attracts most of the people who come to visit. When it comes right down to it, deciding whether one wine is better than another or which characteristics of a wine are the most important (fruit forward vs. earthiness etc.) proves to be quite difficult. Wine professionals and academics have developed tools and techniques (such as aroma wheels and sensory evaluation methodologies) as a means of developing objective criteria to evaluate wines. But they are usually not for the average person with an interest in wine and the Napa Valley. The best way to find out where quality wines are found in the valley is to sample public opinion or ask the experts.

There are several websites on the Internet that have free reviews of wines submitted by the public. They could be useful in identifying wineries to visit, but their databases are often incomplete. There are also the websites of the experts like Robert Parker and the *Wine Spectator* that offer their entire databases of wines they have rated. Of those expert-based websites, the *Wine Spectator's* website (www.winespectator.com) is probably the most complete tool for identifying which wineries exhibiting wine excellence you should consider. Unfortunately, the websites of the experts charge for their information, sometimes much more than it is worth for this exercise. The *Wine Spectator*, though, does offer its entire tasting notes database of more than 222,000 wine reviews. These can be sorted by region, varietal, and vintage, which will yield a list of wines and their ratings and tasting notes. The cost is $49.95 for a year's subscription, but fortunately, the *Wine Spectator* also offers this service on a monthly basis for only $7.95, an amount that is reasonable if it helps to assure a rewarding experience in the Napa Valley. Be apprised that this subscription will be automatically renewed each succeeding month, so if you are using this database only to try and locate wineries to visit on your trip to the Napa Valley, be sure to follow the instructions to cancel the subscription before the month is up.

When you have located several potential wineries to visit, there is the issue of which vintages of the wine they will be pouring. Fortunately, the Napa Valley does not have huge differentials in wine quality from year to year like some wine regions do, but winemakers, and even winery owners, do come and go. And there are always unpredictable factors that cause wine quality to change from year to year. Therefore, it would be wise to call the wineries' tasting room in advance to find out if they are pouring the wine you are interested in, and which vintages. Checking back with the *Wine Spectator* database will confirm that you will be getting the wine experience you were hoping for.

2. Varietal Diversity

Although current public tastes and the *terroir* of the Napa Valley somewhat dictate what varietals are produced and sold by Napa Valley wineries, a very large number of grape varietals are available at valley wineries. Thanks to Robert Mondavi, most wines in the Napa Valley and indeed in all "New World wine regions" are labeled by grape variety, with some exceptions, such as blends. Many grape varietals do not do well in areas of the Napa Valley. Unfortunately, due to the necessities of running both a tasting room and wine club (which demands that a large number of different wines be available to customers), some wineries offer a choice of many varietals that they shouldn't. On the other hand, many wineries own properties or source fruit from areas where given varietals do very well and excellent wine results. Using the *Wine Spectator* database or other similar source, a visitor interested in a particular varietal is able to find Napa Valley wineries that feature wines made from that grape. After selecting a winery featuring that varietal, the visitor should then call their tasting room to make sure they are pouring it, find out the vintage of the wine, and check the rating of that vintage in the *Wine Spectator* database.

3. Innovation

Napa Valley vintners, often working with university researchers working on leading-edge research and technology, have often used innovative approaches to solve problems and find creative ways to practice viticulture and oenology. This continues to be a part of the wine culture of the valley today. If you have determined that learning about innovative technologies and techniques used in the valley is a high priority for you, the Napa Valley Vintners Association's website (www.napavintners.com) sorts its members' wineries by those that offer wine education, those that practice sustainable farming, and those that participate in the Vintners Association's Napa Green program. (This is described on the website as a "program to encourage and assist Napa Valley vintners and grape growers to implement beneficial and verifiable environmental practices through; preserving and enhancing the environment of the Napa Valley, demonstrating a commitment to our community, and providing leadership for the wine industry.")

4. Ambience

There are so many beautiful valley wineries, some with unique architecture, some exhibiting magnificent art, and some with stunning vistas. Almost every visitor to the valley will want to enjoy at least some of the wineries that exhibit the exceptional ambience that is a part of the Napa Valley wine culture. The website www.napavintners.com sorts the Vintners Association member wineries by those with wine caves, unique architecture, gardens, scenic views, art on display, and historic buildings. After identifying wineries with the ambience that appeals to you, you should visit their websites and call their tasting rooms for more information about their ambience and to confirm that they are what you are looking for. A cross-reference of the wine rating, as described in the *Wine Excellence* section of this book's *Afterword*, could unveil one of the Napa Valley's gem wineries.

5. Hospitality

By any measure one could imagine, the Napa Valley has more hospitality than any other wine region in the world. As far as every other attribute of the Napa Valley wine culture is concerned, there are other wine regions of the world that may equal the valley in certain areas, but not in hospitality. If enjoying the warm conviviality of the valley's tasting rooms is a high priority of yours, there are two resources on the Internet to help you. The website www.napavintners.com has a category which identifies member wineries that are off the beaten path, family-run, romantic, or fall into other categories relating to their hospitality facilities. The *San Francisco Chronicle* has for a number of years written reviews on hospitality and tasting rooms in the Napa Valley and other wine regions in California. On the *Chronicle*'s website www.sfgate.com, one can find a number of reviews of hospitality and tasting rooms, which include many wineries with exceptional hospitality facilities and programs.

Index

21st Amendment, 121
Aztecs, 15
Bale, Edward 40, 44, 74, 95, 104
Bale, Caroline 40, 95, 104
Bear Flag Republic, 57
Bear Flag Revolt, 47, 57, 68, 72, 79, 82, 83
Beaulieu Vineyard, 110, 111, 112
Beringer, Fredrick 105, 124
Beringer, Jacob 98, 99, 105
Bidwell, John 52, 56, 78, 79, 81
Bolívar, Simón 29
Brackett, James W. 62
Brannan, Sam 74
Brother Timothy, 112
Californios, 12, 20, 30, 31, 33, 34, 38, 39, 42, 43, 44, 50, 52, 58
Campbell, Leon G. 19, 20, 137
Carson, Kit 9, 35, 45, 46, 47, 76
Casa Madero, 24
Chiles, Joseph 35, 44, 52, 56, 78, 79
Christian Brothers Winery, 112, 113
Clyman, James 8, 9, 46, 53
Columbus, Christopher 9, 14, 15, 23
Coppola, Francis Ford 117, 118, 125, 126
Cortez, Hernando 15, 16, 17, 23
Crane, George Belden 11, 66, 74
Daniel Jr., John 111, 125
Davies, Jack and Jamie 116, 123, 124
Eighteenth Amendment, 110
Fremont, John 47, 76
Fume Blanc, 115
General Law of Expulsion, 42

Gold Rush, 8, 11, 13, 39, 47, 59, 64, 65, 67, 68, 69, 70, 71, 72, 74, 79, 80, 81, 84, 85, 86, 87, 102, 119
Grigsby, John 57, 82, 83
Grigsby-Ide Party, 57, 83
Haraszthy, Agoston 62, 72, 92, 93, 94, 95, 96, 102, 103, 104, 109
Hidalgo, Miguel 29
Ide, William 82
Inglenook, 100, 101, 106, 107, 108, 110, 111, 117, 118, 125
Jerez, 14, 15
Krug, Charles 13, 21, 40, 73, 74, 75, 91, 92, 93, 94, 95, 96, 97, 98, 99, 100, 101, 102, 103, 105, 106, 109, 110, 113, 114, 115, 116, 123, 130
Land Act of 1851, 59, 86
Larkin, Thomas 37
Latour, Georges de 110, 111, 112
Malaga, 15
Marsh, John 77, 78, 79, 81
Martini, Louis 113, 114, 122
Mexican War, 17, 20, 47, 59
Mission, 16, 24, 27, 38
Mission grapes, 16, 24
Mondavi, Peter 122, 123,
Mondavi, Robert 114, 115, 118, 131
Newton, Peter 115
Niebaum, Gustave 13, 73, 94, 96, 97, 100, 101, 106, 108, 110, 111, 117, 118, 125, 126
Osborn, John 11, 63, 74, 84
Patchett, John 11, 62, 63, 65, 74, 84, 95, 96, 104
Pellet, Henry A. 11, 74, 96

Phylloxera, 109, 119
Pope, Julian 8, 9, 53
Prohibition, 108, 110, 111, 112, 113, 114, 116, 120, 121, 122, 123, 124, 125
Pueblo, 27
Rancho, 53, 77, 137
Rancho Caymus, 39, 40, 52
Revolutions of 1848, 86, 87
Robidoux, Antoine 35, 45, 52, 76, 78
Rubicon Winery, 118
Schram, Jacob 13, 73, 94, 97, 98, 99, 104, 105, 110, 116, 123, 124
Schramsberg, 97, 98, 105, 116, 123
Serra, Junipero 7, 10, 17, 18, 19, 21, 25, 27, 31
Smith, Jedediah iv, 35, 45, 46, 53, 100
Squatters, 60
Sutter, John 57, 59, 68, 79, 80, 81, 82, 83, 115

Sutter Home, 115
Tchelistcheff, Andre 112, 113
Thompson, Simpson 11, 62, 63, 75, 84
Thompson, William 74
Ugarte, Juan 25
Vallejo, Mariano 10, 34, 37, 38, 39, 40, 43, 51, 52, 57, 60, 61, 62, 79, 83, 86, 93
Vallejo, Salvador 60, 93, 103
Vignes, Jean-Louis 11, 12, 36, 37
Vitis Vinifera, 23
Walker, Joseph 80
White Zinfandel, 115
Wolfskill, John 40, 49, 50
Wolfskill, William 35, 36, 45, 48, 49, 51, 52, 55
Yerba Buena, 81
Yount, George 7, 8, 9, 10, 11, 12, 34, 35, 36, 37, 38, 39, 40, 44, 45, 46, 48, 50, 51, 52, 53, 55, 56, 58, 60, 61, 65, 73, 76, 79, 86, 96, 108, 120, 137

End Notes

[1] Leon G. Campbell, *Colonial Life in Spanish California During the North American Revolution*, http://www. Americanrevolution.org/cal.html

[2] Ibid

[3] Kathi Brown and Rich Greenfield, *"California as I Saw It": First Person Narratives of California's Early Years 1849-1900* (Washington D.C., Library of Congress, 1977), p.81

[4] Paul K. Kurtkowski, Sonoma Hiking, www.sfgate.com/cgi-bin/article.cgi?file=/gate/archive/2001/03/16/sonomahiking.DTL, 2001

[5] Denzel Verado and Jennie Dennis Verado, *Napa Valley: from Golden Fields to Purple Harvest* (Northridge, Ca.: Windsor Publications, 1986), p.25

[6] Ibid

[7] Ibid

[8] Ibid

[9] Lyman L. Palmer, W.F. Wallace, Harry Laurenz Wells, *The History of Napa and Lake Counties, California etc.*, (1881, San Francisco, Ca: Slocum Bowen) p. 594

[10] Ellen Lambert Wood, *George Yount, Kindly Host of Caymus Rancho*, (San Francisco, Ca., Grabhorn Press, 1941) p. 107

[11] William Heintz, *Wine Country: a History of the Napa Valley* (Santa Barbara, Ca., Capra Press, 1990) p.126

[12] Ibid

[13] Ibid

[14] Kevin Starr, *California a History*, (New York: Modern Library, 2005), p.110

[15] William Heintz, *Wine Country: a History of the Napa Valley* (San Francisco, Ca., Scottwall Associates, 1999) p. 64

[16] Jeff Byrd, Napa Valley History, http://napavalleyrealestate.net/archive/history/history3.html (1999)

[17] William Heintz, *Wine Country: a History of the Napa Valley* (San Francisco, Ca., Scottwall Associates, 1999) p.85

[18] Ibid

[19] Ibid

[20] Ibid

[21] William Heintz, *California's Napa Valley: One Hundred and Sixty Years of Winemaking* (San Francisco, Ca., Scottwall Associates, 1999), p. 33

[22] Ibid

[23] Ibid

[24] Lin Weber, *Old Napa Valley the History to 1900*, (Saint Helena: Wine Ventures Publishing, 1998), p. 254

[25] "California Gold Migration," *New York Herald*, 11 July 1849, p. 93

[26] J.S. Holliday, *Rush for Riches, Gold Fever and the Making of California*, (Berkeley: University of California Press, 1999), p. 88

[27] Ibid

[28] Ibid

[29] William Heintz, *California's Napa Valley: One Hundred and Sixty Years of Winemaking* (San Francisco, Ca., Scottwall Associates, 1999), p.34

[30] Lin Weber, *Old Napa Valley the History to 1900*, (Saint Helena: Wine Ventures Publishing, 1998), p. 214

[31] William Heintz, *California's Napa Valley: One Hundred and Sixty Years of Winemaking* (San Francisco, Ca., Scottwall Associates, 1999), p.34

[32] Denzel Verado and Jennie Dennis Verado, *Napa Valley: from Golden Fields to Purple Harvest* (Northridge, Ca., Windsor Publications, 1986), p.143

[33] Lin Weber, *Old Napa Valley the History to 1900*, (Saint Helena: Wine Ventures Publishing, 1998), p. 214

[34] John Ralston, *Agoston Haraszthy, 1812-1869 Aristocrat, Entrepreneur, Official, Winemaker,* http://www.sfhistoryencyclopedia.com/articles/h/haraszthyAgoston.htm (2004)

[35] Bonnie Phelan (transcriber), Lewis Publishing Company, Memorial and *Biographical History of Northern California,* http:/www.cageenweb.com/archives/Biographies/napa/napa-krug.htm, (2005)

[36] Ibid

[37] Ibid

[38] William Heintz, *California's Napa Valley: One Hundred and Sixty Years of Winemaking* (San Francisco, Ca., Scottwall Associates, 1999), p. 98

[39] Beringer Vineyards, *History and Commitment to Quality,* http://www.beringer.com/Winemaking-Legacy.aspx

[40] Lin Weber, *Old Napa Valley the History to 1900,* (Saint Helena: Wine Ventures Publishing, 1998), p. 249

[41] Ibid

[42] Ibid

Made in the USA
Charleston, SC
14 November 2011